Log Home
SECRETS OF SUCCESS

An Insider's Guide to Making
Your Dream Home a Reality

ROLAND SWEET

PIXYJACK PRESS INC

LOG HOME SECRETS OF SUCCESS:
AN INSIDER'S GUIDE TO MAKING YOUR DREAM HOME A REALITY

Copyright © 2010 by Roland Sweet

Published by PixyJack Press, Inc.   PO Box 149, Masonville, CO 80541 USA

First Edition 2010

9 8 7 6 5 4 3 2 1

ISBN 978-0-9773724-7-8

Library of Congress Cataloging-in-Publication Data
Sweet, Roland.
  Log home secrets of success : an insider's guide to making your dream home a reality /
Roland Sweet. -- 1st ed.
      p. cm.
  Includes index.
  Summary: "Covers designing, planning, building and living in a log home, with details on selecting
a log-home producer, evaluating log packages, incorporating green energy, buying land, calculating
costs, and working with a builder and other key players. Also discusses interior decorating,
landscaping, living with wildlife, log home maintenance, and warranties"--Provided by publisher.
  ISBN 978-0-9773724-7-8
  1. Log cabins--United States. I. Title.

  TH4840.S94 2010
  690'.837--dc22
                                    2010022907

Front cover photo courtesy of Rocky Mountain Log Homes.
Back cover photo courtesy of Maple Island Log Homes.

Book design by LaVonne Ewing.

For Janice, Randy, Diane, Pat & Bob

Those were the days, my friend,
We thought they'd never end.

Contents

INTRODUCTION

This book grew from a series of presentations I began making at log-home shows around the turn of the century. These were three-day events, each attended by several thousand people. Until my speaking debut, my role was to staff a magazine booth near the exit and hawk "current and recent issues," as we called them, at closeout prices. Folks leaving the show would gather and ransack the stacks, looking for anything they thought could possibly help them plan their log home.

Many browsers chatted about the magazines, the shows and log homes. Listening to them, I could tell many knew less on their way out than they thought they'd known when they entered. More precisely, they had been bombarded with so much information that they were confused and unable to comprehend any more. Instead of being enlightened, way too many had become discouraged. I concluded that many were never going to own a log home.

When not working the shows, I was editing *Log Homes Illustrated* magazine, helping fuel people's dreams of owning one of these beautiful wood homes. Its mainstay was lavish photo tours of North America's best log homes, accompanied by interviews with the homeowners. These people were gracious enough to share with me, and in turn our readers, why they wanted a log home in the first place and then how they made theirs happen. They had survived what for most was a trial-and-error process, since, until they built their homes, few had little clue how the process unfolded. Having accomplished what seemed to them like a minor miracle, they were thrilled with their choice of a log home and felt it had added a special joy to their lives.

I couldn't help but wonder what if the people at the shows who were so overwhelmed and discouraged by what lay ahead only knew what the people who already owned log homes had found out and been through. I began poring over my interview notes and found some common threads. These became the basis for my talk: "Planning for Success: 25 Tips to Make Your Log Home Dream Come True."

I also saw that too many people coming through the doors at the shows wandered aimlessly around the exhibit hall. I presumed that everyone attending wanted a log home or at least wanted to see if they wanted a log home. Although log homes were the premise of these shows, as often happens whenever a crowd gathers, certain hucksters staffed booths and touted an array of impulse-buy items: cookware, ladders, magic brooms and super shammies (which, by the way, actually work as advertised, I can testify, having used mine during a storm to soak up rainwater seeping through the allegedly impenetrable tile floor of my den).

It amazed me how many people walked out the door with $4,000 worth of cookware that they obviously hadn't come to the show expecting to buy but did. When I worked up the courage to stop some of these people and ask why they had bought non-log items at a log-home show, the gist of their answers was that they could understand fast-talking cookware, ladder and magic broom sellers, but they couldn't figure what the log-home salespeople were talking about and felt they had to leave with something to justify the time spent there.

I came up with a second presentation: "How to Get the Most from the Show." It sug-gested ways to make sense of the confusion on the show floor so that you stayed on track to get the information you paid for and not feel obligated to settle for a magic broom or cookware, at least not until you had first bought your log home.

That, in a long-winded way, is the origin of this book and my gratitude to the people who inspired me to write it: the hundreds of people who own a log home and the many, many hundreds more who wish they did. Both helped me make my magazine better.

When John Kupferer hired me in 1988 to help him launch *Log Home Living* magazine, he told me something that guided me through the next 22 years: Don't play favorites. It was good advice but not always easy to follow. I knew nothing about log homes at the time, but as I became familiar with them, I found myself not only liking them, but also preferring certain styles and even certain log-home companies. Whenever I felt tempted to indulge my prefer-ences in print, I remembered John's advice.

Remaining objective helped *Log Home Living* and later *Log Homes Illustrated* pres-ent a bigger, truer picture of log homes to our readers. By exploring and revealing the many possibilities, we inspired a lot of people to discover for themselves the delights of living in a log home. Foremost was the opportunity to express their individual ideas of what a log home could be.

Since that eventful beginning, I've visited dozens of log homes and seen photographs of hundreds more. I've yet to see any two alike. Even homes built from the same standard floor plan turn out differently.

This uniqueness underlies the appeal of log homes. Sure, there's the wood, but that's a given. Being able to configure this wood any way you choose matters plenty. And once you begin exploring the possibilities, you find so many that your biggest challenge will likely be deciding which ones are right for you.

Choice is what log homes are all about. I hope this book will inspire you to explore the possibilities for yourself. Log homes have evolved considerably since the 1980s. When I page through back issues of all the log-home magazines that have been published since then, I marvel at how much greater the variety is now. People's tastes have changed, but so have the companies that cater to those tastes. Architects, log-home companies, builders, decorators—all feel lots freer to flex their imaginations and challenge the expectations of their customers.

This book aims not just to help you succeed overall, but also to see you through the preliminaries by revealing what really matters so you won't waste time with what doesn't and can get on with making your dream home happen. For me, John Kupferer's advice not to play favorites worked. Don't apply it to your own quest for the perfect log home, however. Choose the one home you come up with that is your favorite and uniquely yours. Don't settle for anything less.

Roland Sweet
Mount Vernon, Virginia

More than half a million American families enjoy living in their log homes. So can you.

Keep Your Eye on the Prize

1

So you want to buy a log home. Or think you do. Or thought you did—past tense because more than a few people have abandoned their dreams of owning a log home. Who knows why. Maybe they realized a log home wasn't right for them. Or they weren't right for it. Or it just wasn't worth the trouble, time or money.

More than a few dreamers have awakened over the years to what you may just be discovering: Log homes don't come easy. Jim Cooper, who knows more about log homes than most people, having bought, sold, built and lived in them, once observed, "If owning a log home were as easy as walking into a sales representative's office with a floor plan and a checkbook, the hillsides and meadows of America would be blanketed with log homes." Even though Jim wrote a best-selling book called *Log Homes Made Easy*, he's right about their sparsity. There are no log Levittowns.

And yet, more than half a million American families own log homes. People who, by the way, are no smarter, richer or better looking than you. How did they succeed in making their dream come true?

It didn't just happen. They made it happen.

These are the people you would be wise to emulate. After all, if you wanted to make money, you wouldn't seek financial advice from someone who just filed for bankruptcy. Likewise, if you want a log home, heed folks who already own theirs. They've experienced the trial and error you hope to avoid.

I did just that. Many times over. Their answers, distilled into what I call 30 secrets of success, are the basis for this book. Their triumphs can and will help you succeed—if, that is, you genuinely want a log home.

There is no practical reason for building one. Maybe there was in pioneer times, when slapdash shelter was essential for survival on the frontier. Today's log homes are entirely discretionary purchases, however. The reasons anyone today would want one are purely emotional.

People feel passionate about log homes, sometimes to the point of overlooking or ignoring what buying and building one entails. That's why the people who sell log homes perplex me. Many go to great lengths to discourage people who enthusiastically want one. Maybe they think they are being realistic.

Let me make my point by describing a scene I've seen hundreds of times at log-home shows. These shows started in the mid-1990s and over the next 10 years grew to where there were as many as four dozen a

year. I can say without exaggerating that I attended more than a hundred of these shows, meeting everyone with enough interest in log homes to pay the $10-to-$15 admission. These folks ranged from hot prospects to idly curious, but they were all potential buyers, whose emotions were stirred by the notion that they might one day own a log home.

No matter how big or small the show, the exhibit floor features aisles of booths staffed by people selling log homes, presumably for a living. Many—at some shows most—set up static displays of the actual logs their company sells. These are typically corner displays, cutaway wall sections or scaled-down buildings. As show-goers step into or often just approach a booth, a friendly salesperson greets them and, after perfunctory chitchat, begins pointing at these displays and reciting the technical advantages of the company's way of designing and engineering their logs to be assembled.

In most cases, these building systems are pretty sophisticated, beyond most people's ability to comprehend their importance or even if they are important (although they must be because the salespeople go to such lengths to show them in great detail). To complicate technical matters, most every company's engineered building system differs from the others. The salesperson extols the merits of the company's way and embarks on a lengthy, detailed explanation of not only how it works, but also why it works better than every other company's building system.

Now, nobody disputes the need for a building system. Who wants a log home that's going to tumble over? Not that any ever has. But who even knew there were such things? And, when you get right down to it, who cares?

I don't know the intricacies of how my automobile is assembled; I just care that it goes when I step on the gas and that the radio plays loud.

But the sudden barrage of terminology and technology, plus the claim that one system tops all the rest, has a predictable effect on people trying to take it all in, people who simply want to satisfy a passion to own a log home. Their eyes glaze over. Their brains clearly cannot grasp even the basic concept underlying the whole structure. Add to that one, two, maybe three dozen companies whose salespeople all claim their way is best, and you would see, as I did so many times, people shake their heads and walk away. More than once, I actually witnessed the exact moment when their dreams poofed into disappointment.

To give you some idea of how carried away these pitches can get, I've twice (so far) heard salespeople for companies whose names contain the words "log" and "home" declare at educational sessions at log-home shows in front of audiences that anyone who buys a log home is asking for trouble. Folks stampeded for the exit.

The confusing terminology and technology and the contradictory, sometimes outrageous claims that discourage buying a log home don't even hint at what is perhaps the biggest obstacle to owning a log home: building it. In almost every case, log-home companies (also called log-home producers) cut the logs and ship them to buyers' land. Unloaded, unstacked logs offer little clue as to what might be involved in transforming them into a habitable home. Anyone who's ever tried to find a contractor to finish a basement or re-do a kitchen in an ordinary house will appreciate how formidable a task it must be to find an experienced, savvy and reputable log-home builder.

So there's the quandary. A handful of people in the whole United States passionately want a log home and are capable of paying for one, but the system of buying and building it thwarts them.

The challenge may be a far cry from crossing this vast country in a covered wagon, chopping down whatever trees could be found and stacking them to form a cabin for shelter against all forms of peril. In a sense,

"Now, when someone asks if I live in a log home, finally I can answer, 'Yes.' I also can reflect on what I learned: Designing and building a log home is a fascinating, challenging process. It'll take two years out of your life. It's worth it."

Dunstan Family
Garfield County, Colorado

though, the people who succeed in owning a log home today are also pioneers. Their stories are inspiring.

I was fortunate to get to know some of these people and to relate their success stories in the magazines I have edited for more than 20 years: *Log Home Living* and *Log Homes Illustrated*. Both these publications offered plenty of advice to people considering buying and building log homes. Almost all the homeowners I interviewed revealed something they figured out ahead of time or along the way. Or maybe they didn't realize it until they had moved in. Forethought, hindsight, trial and error—it doesn't matter. However they got there, the result is the same: Their dream came true.

Their stories revealed the fundamental truth about log homes. All these people wanted a log home enough that they refused to let the people who sell and build log homes undermine their pursuit of that dream. They overcame the obstacles by understanding at some level the message that I would like to share with you, the message that prompted me to write this book for those of you who sincerely want a log home.

Your goal isn't to buy and build a log home. Your goal is to live in a log home. It sounds so obvious, doesn't it? Yet, it is an underlying principle that people quickly lose sight of once they embark on the path to owning a log home.

Like most worthwhile things in life, reaching your goal means jumping through hoops. Buying a car, putting your kids through school—you can make your own list. Some know-it-alls love to point out that the journey matters more than the destination. OK, but the destination has to be worth the journey, or why set out in the first place?

You can bet the American pioneers heading west who built those crude cabins along the way didn't regard the trek as their reward. Yet, once they got where they were going, many of them no doubt reflected on their experience more favorably than they felt while undergoing it. That will surely be the case once

> "People need to realize, you look at our home and think this is a really nice home, but we all go through sacrifices to have what we have. That's a part of it."
>
> Price Family
> Northwest Arkansas

you are living in your log home. "Misadventures," Emily Post wrote (yes, etiquette maven Emily Post), "afterwards become your most treasured memories."

Just make sure you reach your goal by not losing sight of it. Remember above all: **Half a million American families enjoy living in their log homes. So can you.**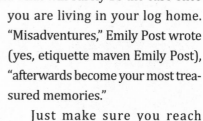

Learn the Common Log Home Myths and Why They Are Myths

2

People who want a log home are often talked out of it by well-meaning but ill-informed friends, who cite plenty of reasons why log homes are a bad choice. Chances are, most of these gloomy Guses have never set foot in a log home and are passing along things that "a friend of a friend" told them—in other words, urban legends. You want to know what log homes are like, talk to people who live in them. They aren't likely to sugarcoat the experience, plus the fact that there are more log-home owners than ex-log-home owners ought to speak for itself.

Do yourself a favor. Thank your friends for caring enough to share the bad news about log homes, but find out the facts for yourself.

Myth: There is one best wood.

Fact: There is NO best wood. Twenty-five species all work satisfactorily. Whichever species of wood your company uses, rest assured that it will work the best with the company's building system to accommodate log movement and be fully compatible with the other components to perform to its very best.

Myth: Log homes are a cheap alternative.

Fact: The quality and substance of the building material and the expertise required to turn it into a finished home make log homes as costly as other custom homes, occasionally more so.

Myth: Log homes require no maintenance because logs come from trees, which nobody has to paint.

Fact: Wood in use, exposed to the elements, must be protected, and that protection requires ongoing vigilance and renewal.

Myth: Log homes aren't energy efficient.

Fact: Logs have a low R-value because these resistance ratings were devised by the manufactured-insulation industry, whereas logs rely on natural insulation, which doesn't translate favorably into R-value. The measure of logs' energy efficiency is thermal mass and actual performance. These criteria attest to the superior energy efficiency of log homes.

Where this efficiency falls down is in poorly designed homes or ones that fail to provide proper insulation around doors and windows and between the walls and the roof. Also, for all the romance and tradition associated with traditional fireplaces, they are inefficient and provide very little heat for the fuel they require. The good news is that several other options (wood stoves, fireplace inserts and masonry stoves) are available today.

Myth: Log homes are a banquet for termites.

Fact: Log homes are no more susceptible to termites or other wood-eating or wood-boring pests than any wood home. But consider that in log homes, the wood is exposed, rather than concealed behind drywall and siding. If termites do make it through your home's defensive measures, the foremost being soil treatment to halt their advance, you will be able to spot their presence before damage results because you can see it.

Myth: Log homes are firetraps.

Fact: Log homes actually resist fire better than stick-built homes, which

The measure of logs' energy efficiency is thermal mass and actual performance.

amount to so much kindling. Log walls tend not to catch fire in the first place, but if they do, the damage is likelier to be limited to charring. This charring actually provides a protective coating for the wood, similar to the effect created by fire-retardant chemicals, and after the fire is extinguished, it can be sanded or blasted off to reveal undamaged, structurally sound wood underneath. What is likely to ignite is non-log materials, usually on the roof or interior, stud-framed walls. Because building density is a factor in spreading fire, the greatest danger to log homes comes from nearby outbuildings, especially ones used to store combustible materials.

"Over the years," the Technical Committee of the Log Homes Council found, "there have been many reports of fires that have burned inside and outside of log buildings without destroying the building's structural integrity, illustrating the fire-resistive nature of solid-wood walls. It is a combination of the insulating response of the charred wood at the surface with the slow rate at which flame will spread along the wood surface, and the fact that there are no concealed cavities in a log wall through which the fire may travel (ultimate fireblocking!). Combined with the selection of beam and deck second-floor and roof options often incorporated into log buildings, log structures are a top choice for endurance and integrity in a fire."

Myth: Log homes are dark and dreary.

Fact: They were when the pioneers built them, but thanks to advances in design, engineering and glazing, today's log homes are usually bathed in natural light. Homeowners' insistence on colorful furnishings has also brightened interiors, as has the tendency of some to incorporate drywall inside homes to reflect light throughout.

Myth: Log homes can't be insured.

Fact: They can, and the ones that can't tend to pose risks independent of whether they're log. For instance, most log homes are built in rural settings, where fire departments are staffed by volunteers who have less sophisticated fire-fighting equipment and usually need to bring water to the site because rural homes tend not to have fire hydrants. Also, as a result of their rural settings, log homes may be at risk of wildfires, although log homes have proven reliable in withstanding not just fires, but also natural disasters that may reduce their non-log neighbors to rubble.

Keep in mind that insurance companies don't act as a monolith. Companies assess risk differently. If one company won't insure your log home, try another. Your lender or log-home sales representative ought to be able to recommend insurers that have covered previous homeowners. But before you build your home, you owe it to yourself to find out who will provide coverage.

These are just the most common raps against log homes that derive from ignorance. Any others you may hear, do yourself a favor and investigate them to come up with the truth. One thing that is amazing is the number of myths spread by log-home company salespeople in their zeal to win you over to their product by assuring you that other companies are inferior. A few sales may result, but it's far more likely that potential customers respond to this negative-sell message with suspicion that all log homes are inferior. What makes their misrepresentations discouraging and dangerous is that they aren't uninformed friends thinking they're doing you a favor. They're people who should know better and people you should steer clear of.

Understand Wood 3

Keeping focused on your goal of living in a log home won't always be easy. Distractions abound, not just from the other events and activities going on in your life, but also from the process of getting your log home. It's quite possible to wander off down one of these sidetracks and never return. One of the most tempting is the quest to find the best wood for your log home.

Presumably, the reason you want a log home is because it's made of wood. If wood isn't why you want a log home, now might be a good time to trade in this book for *The Insider's Guide to Vinyl Siding*, rather than read all the way through and conclude that everything about log homes makes perfect sense except the part about the wood. That's why this step is way up front, so you'll get a sense of what wood is all about before you commit to owning a log home.

When we talk about a log home, we don't mean boards, what are known as dimensional lumber or, dismissively, sticks. We're talking solid wood that looks less like lumber and more like tree trunks. In fact, these tree trunks are the premise of logs.

So far, so good. Now imagine you start talking to several log-home companies and learn that one

of them sells cedar logs, another pine logs. Another sells cypress logs. Another sells oak logs. Another sells larch logs. Yet another sells pine and cedar logs at the same time. And the ones that sell pine logs sell different kinds of pine. This predicament is understandably perplexing, like trying to choose the right cough medicine in a drugstore, only with considerably more at stake.

If you begin researching different kinds of wood, you'll open up new questions about tensile strength, density, slope of grain and an array of other attributes. If you get really caught up in pursuing which wood is the best for the logs in your log home, you might well feel compelled to enroll at a university and study wood science. Wood has become your new life's pursuit, not living in a log home.

Even a degree in wood isn't going to answer the question of which is the best wood to build your log home, however. The reason your quest is doomed to fail is simple: **There is no best wood to build a log home.**

Don't misunderstand. Different species have different characteristics. Some of these traits directly pertain to how the wood performs as part of a log wall. Others have to do with non-structural features, such as looks or price.

Consider, though, that if one wood were the absolute best, every log-home company would have to use that species or face a competitive disadvantage. The fact that these log producers use different woods ought to tell you that none is the best. They make their choice according to which species they can get an ample supply of to meet their needs. Sometimes the determining factor is proximity, other times cost. Log producers tend to

Miracle Wood

Some companies tout certain wood species (invariably the kind they sell) as naturally decay resistant. These claims have some validity when talking about the living tree. All trees produce natural toxins that help them resist attack from fungi and insects. Some trees are more resistant than others. The degree of resistance is determined by the amount and content of toxins that are present in the wood. The highest concentration of naturally produced toxins occurs in the heartwood; the older the tree, the more concentrated the toxins are. Species containing more heartwood than sapwood are much more naturally resistant. Sapwood of all trees has very little to no resistance to insect and decay damage.

Wood species vary in their natural ability to resist decay. Species known to have been used in log construction whose heartwood is resistant or very resistant to decay, according to the Forest Products Laboratory, are old-growth baldcypress, cedar, chestnut, black locust, white oak, old-growth redwood and black walnut.

Moderately resistant species include young-growth baldcypress, Douglas fir, honeylocust, Western larch, swamp-chestnut oak, old-growth Eastern white pine, young-growth redwood, old-growth Southern and longleaf pine, and tamarack.

Slightly resistant or nonresistant species include aspen, firs, hemlock, red and black oak, pines (other than those previously listed), poplar and spruce.

Note that decay resistance is only one characteristic of wood species and has little if any bearing on whether one particular wood is better suited for log construction than another.

In short, there are no miracle woods. All logs used in house construction require periodic application of non-leaching preservatives to protect against fungi and insects—even Western red cedar and cypress, the two most highly promoted, naturally resistant wood species. Southern yellow pine is among the least naturally resistant, and yet it responds to treatment with preservatives, especially pressure treatment, better than most other wood. (A detailed guide to protecting your logs appears at the end of this book.) ⚘

be located near where trees grow, not necessarily right next store to their own forest but somewhere in the vicinity. Companies in Maine generally use logs from the forests of Maine. Companies in Montana favor species that grow in Montana—or rather they did when those species were available. Most still use the same species, only now they may ship them in from Canada or neighboring states because these are the kinds of wood they know will perform the way they expect and prefer.

Pine, which is readily available everywhere in the United States, is generally the cheapest wood for log construction. Western red cedar is considered the premium wood, but because it is native to the Northwest, transporting Western red cedar logs to the East adds substantially, sometimes prohibitively, to the cost.

"We ordered our logs, with a preference for 12-inch timbers, but our builder found a source of 14- to 15-inch standing-dead white pine. We really liked the look and feel of the larger timbers."

Fowler Family
Colville, Washington

The point is that companies use whatever wood works for them. Now, if you are fond of a certain species or are absolutely certain that one particular wood is the very best, for any or no reason other than that you want it, by all means, find a company that offers that wood. But if you don't have a preference and aren't inclined to spend a lot of time answering the question of which wood is best because you're more interested in reaching your goal of living in a log home, then don't worry about it. Concentrate instead on finding a log producer whom you like doing business with and accept whatever wood that company offers, confident that it knows what it is doing. Keep in mind when choosing your log-home producer, however, that most companies will, for a price, obtain any wood species you specify.

While it doesn't help to worry about which wood is best, it doesn't hurt to know a little about wood in general. There's no shortage of information. Wood is a fundamental fabric of civilization. If you want to delve into wood's technical nature, two books that offer comprehensible information are R. Bruce Hoadley's *Understanding Wood* and the U.S. government's *Wood Handbook: Wood As an Engineering Material*.

These books will tell you that wood is a cellular material that makes up the bulk of the tree. Water, tannins, waxes, gums, starches, alkaloids and oils occupy the cell cavities, contributing to the color, odor, taste, decay resistance and flammability of the wood. It is like a honeycomb composed mainly of dead, hollow, tubular cells. This cellular structure is what gives wood its amazing strength and insulating value, and allows it to hold water, oxygen and nutrients.

That succinct scientific description doesn't hint at wood's wonder, however. What attracts you to a log home probably isn't the alkaloids or the tubular cells. The real appeal of this miraculous material goes beyond its physiological nature. It's the many ways people have figured out how to use wood. You'd probably rather read a book that recounts the history of wood from a building and tool perspective. Here's one you can breeze through in an evening and not have to look up any of the words in a dictionary: *A Reverence for Wood* by Eric Sloane. This delightful account of the history and philosophy of woodworking in America will only momentarily distract you from your goal of living in a log home. In fact, it's very likely to deepen your commitment and enthusiasm to reach your goal even sooner. ❀

A Sound Choice

Log homes are a sound idea. That's because solid-wood walls listen well. Science proves it, but you don't need math and graphs to show what your ears tell you: Log homes kill noise and enrich sound.

Logs are thick enough to insulate against distracting background noise, so we can devote our full auditory attention to wonderful music or the human voice or perhaps rain pattering your metal roof. Or maybe just the quiet. Logs are like jumbo Bose noise-canceling headphones for your whole house.

Indoors, log homes control sounds. Or they would if not for changing tastes. Open layouts, popular for promoting a casual air, let sound wander. Partition walls baffle sound, but many log-home buyers shun logs for interiors, preferring drywall because they appreciate decorating versatility.

Less wood in a log home, by the way, isn't most men talking. Guys' idea of decorating a log wall is: Why? It's a log wall. But some men and many women like inside walls white because they're used to it. More might prefer logs, however, if they thought less about looking and more about listening.

Solid-wood walls can turn a room, or even a corner of a room, into a cozy concert hall. Try to visualize log interior walls as decorating schemes for your ears.

Wood absorbs vibrations and filters sound, meaning logs amplify music and the human voice without echo. Sound experts know that the greater the mass of the wall, the greater the sound energy required to set it in motion. The law of mass states that every doubling of the mass of a partition will result in a 6-decibel reduction in the level of sound transmitted through it.

Imagine how much mass fits into solid-wood walls 8 to 12 inches thick. According to "Sound Transmission & Log Walls," a technical note prepared for the Log Homes Council, "The acoustical benefits of a log wall are the reduced transmission provided by its solid mass and the sound deflection provided by the profile of the log (the angle, shape and texture of the log surface)." This report explains these benefits by referring to STC ratings, which apply to construction methods and materials that isolate and insulate noise.

The STC (Sound Transmission Class) is a "numeric value generated by the methods described in ASTM E413-73 Standard Classification for Determination of Sound Transmission Class," which, the report reads, "is designed to correlate with subjective impressions of the sound insulation provided against the sounds of speech, radio, television, music and similar sources of noise in offices and dwellings." Ratings range from 0 to 70. You can hear loud conversation through a wall with a 30 rating, but a 50-rated wall blocks the sound.

Stud walls, the LHC tech note says, "rely on

thin exterior sheathing and siding to reflect the sound, add an interior wallboard that traps air in the cavity to buffer sound, then add insulation in the wall cavity. Research has shown that the connection between layers of materials affects transmission, and that cavity construction uses the airspace to reduce transmission."

The report points out that no tests have been performed on log walls, so no STC rating can be assigned. But, it declares, "the fact that log walls use the density of the solid wood to limit transmission cannot be denied. Add the experience of those who live or work in log buildings—outside noise is not an issue."

And indoors? As you design spaces, listen to your ears for direction. "Hard surfaces, such as log walls, wood floors and glazing may be desirable to reflect voices and music," the LHC tech note says. "Softer or textured surfaces may absorb sound while obstacles can disperse sound instead of reflecting it."

So, log homes enhance voices, not just music. Basso booms even more profundo. Not just singers, but silver-tongued orators also sound golden. Even humdrum conversation in a log home seems downright dramatic.

It all has to do with what scientists call wood's acoustical properties. "The same qualities that provide better thermal value," the LHC tech note says, "also perform better acoustically."

Prehistoric people discovered wood's performance qualities the first time they banged a log and heard it resonate. Since then, it's been all refinement. "Dry wood," states the government's *Wood Handbook: Wood As an Engineering Material*, "is an incomparable material for such musical instruments as the violin."

The proof is Stradivarius violins, not so much for Antonio Stradivari's workmanship as for their wood. As the *Wood Handbook* puts it: "Variability in the speed of sound in wood is directly related to the variability of modulus of elasticity and density."

Wikipedia indicates Stradivari used spruce for the harmonic top of his violins, willow for the internal parts and maple for the back, strip and neck. What's more, he treated the wood with potassium borate (borax), sodium and potassium silicate, and vernice bianca, a varnish comprising Arabic gum, honey and egg white. (Borates, by the way, are a naturally occurring wood preservative commonly used to protect wall logs.)

Theories abound as to where Stradivari obtained his wood. One is that he used very, very old wood from the "little ice age." This notion stems from the wood's high density, which was ideal for making stringed instruments. Trees that grew during this period contained tree rings that were closer together and denser than those produced in more temperate conditions.

Another possibility Wikipedia mentions is that the wood came from the forests of northern Croatia. This wood, called Javor, is known for its extreme density due to the slow growth from harsh Croatian winters. Croatian wood was a commodity traded by Venetian merchants of this era and still favored by local lutheirs for crafting musical instruments.

Bagpipes lack the nuance of violins, but Scotland's national instrument also depends on wood for its characteristic clamor. African Blackwood has been used to make Highland pipes since Scottish mariners began bringing it back from Africa in the 18th century. It replaced the native bog oak because it made a sweeter sound.

Wood aids hearing, too. Syracuse University's Belfer Audio Laboratory and Archive built a live-end, dead-end (LEDE) studio to assure authentic reproduction of its collection of 340,000 sound recordings on wax, tin foil, paper, shellac, vinyl, tape and other media since Edison. Forsaking modern synthetic sound-enhancing materials, it relied on wood.

Incidentally, the irony of Edison inventing sound recording is that he was deaf. "So he would listen by biting into the wood of the recording machine, because he could hear by bone conduction," Richard Koprowski of Stanford University's *Archive of Recorded Sound* says. Again: wood.

The LEDE principle applies to home listening. Generally, you want to hear only the direct sound coming from the instrument or speakers, with no influence or coloration by the room's acoustics. To prevent stray reflections, the wall areas behind and directly adjacent to the speakers are designed to absorb sound to provide a "dead" end to the room. The opposite or back wall is left "live" and diffuses any standing sound waves within the room, creating a small gap between the time of arrival of the direct sound and the arrival of the first highly diffused sound from the live end. This technique, audio experts say, creates a cleaner listening environment with better sound clarity, improved stereo imaging and smoother frequency response.

Logs enrich sound because they possess the same acoustical properties as govern wooden instruments and sound studios. So, if you prefer Surround Sound to any old noise around, logs will naturally enhance your acoustic experience. Creating a paradise for your ears adds to the sensory enjoyment of log-home living. ❀

Think Green

America is going green. Because green matters, you're probably wondering whether logs are green. Of course they're green, or I wouldn't raise the issue. But green living goes beyond the logs and the way they're turned into a home.

First, though, what does "green" mean? The term has gone from a social movement to a marketing slogan. But the underlying ethic of green thrives: sustainability, renewability, conscientiousness. Green goes beyond clichés. Simply put: The goal of green is conservation. Ground-bound resources are limited. Green ultimately postpones our extinction.

The fact that your home will be built of logs is a very big start to going green. Any kind of home can be green, but log-home buyers enjoy an edge.

First, logs are a renewable resource.

Second, you're starting from scratch, with a brand-new home, rather than retrofitting and jerry-rigging. So you can do it right the first time with high-quality windows, well-insulated roof, etc.

Third, you'll be living more among nature than apart from it.

Fourth, like nine out of every ten log-home owners, you'll be building your home on raw land. You're able to buy the right site and position it on the most advantageous spot on that site, whether to benefit from sunshine (passive solar heat) or thwart hostile winds.

Fifth, you have incentive to use longer-lasting materials and install efficient mechanical systems because you'll likely be living longer in your log home and will enjoy their full value, as well as recoup your cost.

Sixth, you'll likely be building your home in the country. Remoteness from the power grid suggests investigating alternative energy, traditionally solar and wind power or some combination (unless you have a year-round stream running through your property that you can tame for micro-hydroelectric power). Not to be overlooked is geothermal heat pumps, an excellent method for heating and cooling homes. More on this at the end of the chapter.

All of these tie in nicely with the best solution of choosing to live simpler. A log home encourages stepping back from powered things, a little or a lot. It's an idyllic image, but at a more down-to-earth level, going green pays off.

It also costs. That's why many log-home companies offer green as an option, making it clear to customers that they're paying more for that choice. Green's payback comes down the road.

You'll find out that log-home companies don't all mean the same thing when they offer green. There are no standards for green, but just as standards appeared for organic food, expect them sooner than later. Log-home companies are aware of the inevitability of standards and their adherence to, and the responsible companies are reading up on and even helping develop these standards.

Standards do apply to certain materials and appliances that you may use in your log home. Energy-efficiency ratings are easily comparable. Look for those yellow appliance tags or comparison shop at *www.energystar.gov*.

Any kind of new home lets you choose the latest smart-house technology. Go as green as you're willing to commit to. But here are some features of green that are also more common in log homes than ordinary homes.

"By adding two levels of logs to elevate the walls, we raised the porch roof higher than the windows to admit more light underneath and expose the views from the inside. Another effect was to raise the height of the upstairs walls, allowing for bigger windows and for more headroom without going to dormers. We get sunlight in the house all day. People walk in, and they can't believe how bright it is."

Forget Family
Gloucester, Rhode Island

The Logs

Still worth repeating: Logs are renewable. Not quid pro quo, however. We're replacing forest trees with farmed trees. There's the same amount of wood fiber from an industrial standpoint, but not a lot of biodiversity from a habitation standpoint. At least no rainforests are pillaged for house logs, and farmed species mature quicker and get renewed more often.

A desirable alternative, even though non-renewable, log resource is trees in forest that have been killed by pests or wildfires. These trees died on the stump but were left standing, either because they're too deep in the woods or too spread apart to make harvesting them profitable. These trees are called dead standing, standing dead, dried on the stump. Whatever you call them, they make good logs, especially out West, where millions of acres of beetle-killed standing-dead, nicely dried pine could be turned into log homes a lot longer than oil's going to be in the ground. As civilization's luck would have it, pine-destroying beetles are teeming farther and wider

Even on cold winter days, passive solar heating from the south-facing wall of windows provide substantial warmth for this mountain log home.

than ever, thanks to global warming's expanding their range into forests too cold for them to survive before.

Wildfires also produce standing-dead trees. Usually these fires roar through living trees so quickly that only the needles and outer branches, especially at the top, are destroyed. The tree dies, but the trunk is merely charred. Removing that burned outer layer is the same as any log mill would do to a freshly harvested log still loaded with moisture and in some cases sap resin. Beautiful logs were turned out from trees killed by the great Yellowstone Fire of 1988. So, there's a steady supply of standing-dead trees. Best of all, the remaining trees will likely re-seed a lot of the newly cleared space, assuring greater diversity.

Logs' natural insulating ability also saves on using manufactured wrapped or blown-in insulation material made by chemical companies. And the fact that log homes favor open floor plans means fewer partition walls and better flow of heat and air.

A couple other green considerations: buying logs locally saves transportation cost; logs are solid wood, and solid wood prevents vapor diffusion, which carries moisture into wall cavities and traps it there unless you allow for drying.

SIPs

Structural insulated panels are a great energy saver especially suited for log homes. Not the walls, obviously. But SIPs use foam cores and glue, neither of which seems particularly easy on the environment. But they also recycle wood chips and increase the energy efficiency of buildings tremendously.

SIPs gained popularity with timber framers as wall sheathing. As SIP technology improved, the panels found favor in general construction. Log builders were slow to adopt SIPs because logs pretty much took care of the wall material and achieved better-than-average energy efficiency.

As emphasis on energy efficiency intensified, studies demonstrated that the weak link in log and every other home that isn't a cave is the roof. Conventional homes overcome this weakness by shoring up insulation in

Being green addresses the following areas:

▶ *Home Design*

▶ *Site Planning*

▶ *Water Usage*

▶ *Energy Efficiency*

▶ *Materials Used*

▶ *Indoor Air Quality*

the attic beneath the roof. Log homes were hard-pressed to follow this method because of the prevalence of open, rafter-and-purlin ceilings. SIPs overcame the problem by providing a topping that allowed open ceilings while boosting the upper-air R-value. SIPs block rising warmth's escape and, when combined with ceiling fans, greatly increase room comfort while reducing heating costs.

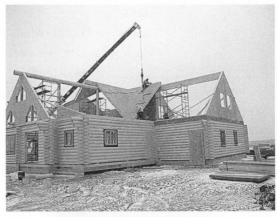

SIP improvements continue, not just the energy efficiency of the panels, but also the environmental friendliness of their composition and production.

Setting SIPs roof panels on a log home (top photo), and the finished ceiling.

Natural Materials

Log homes typically use stone for chimneys and foundation facing, but also for flooring, countertops, even roofing. All are great uses of another green material.

Log lovers are also wood lovers, meaning they tend to favor wood furniture and flooring. A lot of the wood furniture in log-homes is heirlooms or antiques, lessening demand for newly made items, thereby conserving resources.

It doesn't help that many healthy trees are turned into lawn and garden mulch, a natural product for sure but hardly an environmentally friendly one. And certainly not the landscaping necessity their producers try to make us believe. Log homes encourage natural settings, favoring low-maintenance ground cover over lawns that use mulch. Think mulch isn't anti-green because it's made from tree bark, not the whole trees? Barkless trees die. And a major competitor for cypress logs is mulchers, who grind up cypress trees and charge a premium price. One reason to build your home from cypress logs is to keep the mulchers from getting it.

Glass

The popularity of big windows in log homes opens up views, but also lets in light. Natural light uses no electricity. Direct sunlight opens up passive-solar opportunities, from south-facing windows to trombe walls and air-circulation systems to circulate heated air from a sun room or sunny side throughout the house. Today's super-efficient windows also enhance the look of log homes. Skylights and light tubes are also excellent ways to let in natural light and save on electricity.

To learn more about the best windows for your part of the country, and all about low-e windows, UV coatings, gas-filled windows, and more, check out Efficient Windows Collaborative online at *www.efficientwindows.org.*

> "One little touch that worked out well was to put a window in the master bedroom walk-in closet. It's so wonderful getting natural light in a closet. It's so bright and cheery, and you can tell navy from black."
>
> Keeton Family
> Bronson, Florida

A final word about green housing. It's a growing field, driven by innovation. Jumping on the green bandwagon is OK, but be careful which wagon you board. Do your homework and find what works best for you and your budget. ❀

Excellent natural daylight is provided by these skylights which can be opened for ventilation.

Renewable Energy Overview

by Rex A. Ewing

Renewable energy is being embraced by log-home owners across the country, from small single component systems to complex hybrid systems. With substantial financial incentives available from the federal government (in the form of tax credits) as well as many local and state utilities and agencies, the payback has never been better. Do your resesrach first and you'll be one step (or several steps) closer to self-sufficiency.

Solar Energy

If you want to create your own electricity from the sun, there are three main types of photovoltaic systems available. Off-grid systems give you total independence from the utility grid; you will need a solar array (mounted on the ground, on your roof, anywhere that faces south without trees blocking the sunshine), a few extra pieces of electrical equipment, batteries to store the energy and a backup generator (propane or gas-fired). Grid-tied systems with battery backup are essentially the same but you will be connected to the grid so you can sell back your extra electricity. Direct grid-tied systems are the simplest configuration and do not have batteries. Your meter will run backwards when you sell those extra watts to the utility company (if they allow it). When checking with your local utility to see if they'll accept your electricity, ask them about net-metering, which simply means that your electricity is worth as much to the utility as theirs is to you.

Wind Energy

For homeowners with at least an acre of land, small, home-based wind turbines are available in various sizes (typically 800 to 1,500 watts), with towers in heights from 30 to 120 feet. But wind is not for everyone. You'll need to do your homework on the viability of wind power for your home site and look into county regulations and neighborhood covenants before making the decision.

Micro-Hydro Energy

Micro-hydro is deal for anyone who has a year-round stream. For a successful micro-hydro installation you

A North Carolina log home powered by roof-mounted PV array.

will need a good volume of water; a good drop in altitude from where the water is diverted to where it runs through the turbine (this is known as "head"); and close proximity to the house. Any turbine manufacturer can run an analysis on the data you gather and give you a pretty good idea of your proposed system's output. Then, if the numbers are good, call the county just to make sure they'll let you do it.

Solar Water Heating (Solar Thermal)

For many households, solar hot water may be a better, more productive place to put your hard-earned dollars than solar electricity. In most North American climates a modest (under $7,000) solar hot water system will supply 70 to 80 percent of a typical family's hot water needs per year. A solar hot water system should pay for itself in less than 10 years. Various types of collectors are available (batch, flat plate, evacuated tubes) for open- and closed-loop systems. You'll want to take into consideration where the collectors will be installed (roof or ground-mounted), freeze-proofing, and where

Solar water heating with evacuated tubes.

the storage tank will be located in the house. Huge systems can be designed for home heating, but most systems are sized to provide domestic hot water for showers, clothes washing, etc. Combine this technology with an on-demand water heater for a highly efficient setup.

Geothermal Heating & Cooling

Ground-source heat pumps (GHPs) are gaining in popularity with more and more qualified installers popping up around the country. These systems use the earth to heat and cool your home. They are silent and non-polluting, but they do require electricity to run the heat exchanger pumps. There are two basic types of underground pipe systems—open loop and closed loop—with several variations. The one you install will depend on where you live, how much land you have, and the characteristics of the soil and ground water. Up to three times more efficient than conventional home heating methods, a GHP system can easily pay for itself in 10 to 20 years. ⚛

MORE INFORMATION:
- *www.dsireusa.org* (for researching rebates, incentives and tax credits)
- *www.EnergyStar.gov*
- *www.FindSolar.com* (to find renewable energy installers in your area)
- *www.NAHBgreen.org*
- *Got Sun? Go Solar 2nd Edition: Harness Nature's Free Energy to Heat & Power Your Grid-Tied Home* by Rex A. Ewing
- *Crafting Log Homes Solar Style: An Inspiring Guide to Self-Sufficiency* by Rex & LaVonne Ewing

Do Your Homework

5

Having identified your goal and determined the premise of your home (namely, the building material) and pointed out some planetary benefits to consider as you plan your log home, it's time to explain the practical steps to log-home ownership promised by this book's title. The path to log-home ownership can be short, long or circuitous. The surest way to complete the journey is to prepare for it.

Successful log-home owners emphasize above all else the importance of research to learn all that's involved and exactly what to expect when buying and building for your log home. The more you know, the better able you'll be to decide what you want.

Simply put, find out everything you might possibly need to know to make your home happen. You can tailor log homes to your taste, your site, your lifestyle, and make them a true expression of yourself. To make the best choice, you owe it to yourself to select from the broadest range of possibilities.

Twenty years ago, not many people knew log homes existed outside of re-creations of pioneer settlements and historic places. Far fewer people than now wanted a log home, and those that did found resources to help them lacking. The appearance of log-home magazines (*Muir's Original Log Home Guide, Log Home Living, Log Home Design Ideas, Log Homes Illustrated* and *Country's Best Log Homes*) and books provided objective information that de-mystified the process.

Jim Cooper's 1993 book, *Log Homes Made Easy*, quickly became required reading. It was followed by some wonderful idea-and-picture books,

many by Cindy Thiede, that depicted inspiring variations on the log-home theme, as well as fundamentals for designing and decorating individual homes.

The log-home companies, understanding the value of an informed consumer, began publishing catalogs that went beyond showing their standard plans and explained what log homes were all about, at least from their point of view. They continued their educational role by exhibiting at log-home shows, which emerged in the mid-1990s. The shows gave consumers the opportunity to see at one time what many log-home companies had to offer and to get answers to their questions about how to obtain one of these homes.

Then came the Internet. Any veteran log-home salesperson will tell you that today's log-home buyer comes better prepared than ever before. Google "log homes," and you can spend years rummaging through all the web sites that provide information. Is it unbiased? Is it beneficial? That's for you to decide. But it's there nonetheless.

Today, the magazines, books, the shows and the Internet combine to provide the fundamentals you'll want to know. If it all seems overwhelming, spend $20 on Jim Cooper's book (the revised third edition, published in 2008, includes new information on green construction techniques and materials) and another $10 for a copy of the latest *Log Home Living Annual*

Buyer's Guide. These two publications, plus this one (which I presume you bought rather than are reading for free in a café bookstore), will acquaint you with most everything you need to know to understand what buying and building a log home takes and to make an informed choice.

Some people disdain the way log homes are sold and built—the whole kit concept, having to find a builder, having different people handle different aspects of the project. This breakdown has a big advantage, however: It lets you control every aspect to make decisions that are best for you.

Having lots of choices isn't a bad thing. After all, owning a log home is a choice. Yours isn't going to be a cookie-cutter home. ✾

"We liked the idea of having a combination of finishes on the interior. On each side of the central full-log structure are standard frame-constructed wings with log veneer on the exterior."

Portu Family
Northern Minnesota

Large eaves and covered decks provide excellent year-round protection.

Getting the Most from the Log Home Shows

og-home shows are the ideal place to get a sense of what lies ahead, both your choices and the process of getting a log home, because you have actual exhibits to help you see what the building material looks like, make comparisons of the different styles and talk to company representatives in person. When you realize that your average log home costs anywhere from $300,000 to $600,000, paying $10 or $15 to find out what's involved seems like such a small investment (and it is tax-deductible once you actually build the home).

Naturally, the log-home companies are trying to interest you in buying a log home, but they're also there to explain to you what log homes are all about. They have pictures and floor displays to point out the many facets of log-home construction, as well as floor plans and designs.

But here's an overlooked point. The shows don't charge admission to make money so much as to keep out the idly curious. Log-home shows aren't the toothpick buffet at Costco. If your aim is to discuss making your log home happen with people who can help you, you don't want freebie families clogging the aisles and exhibitors' booths with random purposelessness. By charging enough to discourage gawkers, the shows ensure that everyone can concentrate on log homes.

Here are some specific tips for getting the most from a log-home show:

As you walk the show floor, look for three things: ideas and information, but also inspiration. Get excited! Keep in mind that everyone at the show can help you toward your goal, even if only to show you what you don't want.

Identify why you're here and what you expect to get from the show. This will depend on where you are in the home-buying process. Are you just curious about what log homes are? Know what they are, think you want one and are just browsing for ideas you can use to plan yours? Have your land and looking for the perfect floor plan and other design ideas? Have a specific plan, maybe even construction drawings, and just want a realistic price estimate? Have everything you need to get going but need a builder? The stage you're at will determine the questions you ask the exhibitors. Getting ahead of yourself will only complicate matters and doubtlessly confuse you.

Have a rough idea of your budget so companies can steer you in the right direction. It's also an eye-opening experience to see just how much log home you can afford. Whatever unfolds, don't expect to buy a home at the show. These are not impulse purchases. The process of buying a home is involved, so take your time and get it right.

Get your bearings. Survey the show floor. Target exhibitors who sell the home you're hoping to buy. Maybe you've familiar with their name from ads, web sites or homes featured in the magazines. Note which exhibitors you want to see and visit them first. Don't get distracted along the way. If you see something interesting, jot down the location and return later.

Before heading out, write down the questions weighing most heavily on your mind. Refer to your notes when you're in each booth so you'll ask the questions that are important to you. Just as important, write down the answers. They'll help you evaluate companies to decide which one is right for you.

Don't rush from booth to booth. Linger and listen, both to other people's questions and the answers.

After visiting exhibitors you wanted to see, then visit others. Be open-minded. Don't overlook exhibitors whose style of home doesn't

initially appeal to you. They may have a great floor plan or answer a question that will help your home-buying experience. And you may find that as you become more familiar with this style of home, it turns out to be your favorite.

Bring several sturdy tote bags with you to carry all the materials you'll find. Better yet is a backpack. Best of all is a rolling carry-on bag. Remember that you're here to educate yourself and make an informed choice by gathering ideas and information. So collect photos, brochures and any other printed material you can carry. Most exhibitors have floor plans for all sizes and budgets. If you don't see something, ask.

Ask lots of questions, but never forget: You are in a sales environment. Be alert for conflicting claims and assurances that one company's way is right and all other ways are wrong. You must be the judge. Exhibiting companies have different ways of producing and selling their homes. They all believe in their building system and are eager to tell you its advantages. They all claim their way is the best. You wouldn't want to deal with a company that didn't believe in what it sells, but such claims and the differences among companies confuse many buyers. Don't get sidetracked worrying about what's best. Instead, discover what's right for you. Most decisions pertaining to your choice of home are matters of personal preference, NOT RIGHT OR WRONG.

Get to know local dealers. Companies at the shows come from all over North America. Don't worry whether they can deliver a log home to your neck of the woods. They wouldn't be at the show if they couldn't. Regardless of where companies are located, many people representing these companies at this show are local dealers. They are a particularly good resource for designing, building and financing your home because they've already sold homes to people who needed these services. Maybe they can even provide these services themselves. If you don't yet have your land, they can even help you find just what you're looking for. Most dealers have sales models or show their customers' houses by appointment. It can be a real incentive seeing what this wonderful building material looks like after it's turned into a finished and furnished log home.

Attend as many educational sessions as interest you. Each is geared toward providing information to help guide your choices. Speakers are all experts in their fields.

When you get home, review everything you learned and all the material you gathered. Organize the confusion. Use file folders, whatever works for you. Save general features and details within larger photos. ✾

Gather Ideas

6

How does gathering ideas differ from doing your homework? Well, doing your homework helps you see the big picture, everything that's involved in buying and building log homes. Gathering ideas starts you on the road to buying and building *your* particular log home.

Owning any log home is a process. It begins with wanting one and ends with living in one. In between is getting one. This middle part of the process is the most involved and requires the most commitment. A vital and exciting part of getting your log home is gathering ideas. This is the dreaming phase of owning a log home. It's fun and costs little. This stage can last for months or even years.

Many people who start out wanting a log home wind up never progressing beyond this stage. Owning a log home becomes one of the many deferred dreams, but their lives turn out just fine without one. Assuming you aspire to go beyond daydreaming, however, let's look at how to gather ideas productively.

Download pictures from the Internet. Most photos and sketches you come across online can be saved as PDF files. Set up a folder on your desktop. Sort through it periodically because as you see more, your preferences will change. Don't delete images showing what you no longer like, in case you change your mind down the road. Instead, move them into a

separate discard folder, either on your desktop or, if memory is an issue, on a DVD.

Read and clip magazines. Not just the log-home magazines, but any magazines that explain custom-home planning and show pictures of room layouts, features and furnishings that appeal to you. But know what you're looking for. Many people label file folders by rooms, then sort them periodically as their preferences change.

Take your own pictures. Your cell phone camera will do for most. After all, you aren't trying to publish them in a glossy magazine or even on a web site, just stash them in an idea file. Two places you'll definitely want to take pictures are home shows and open houses. The shows are also great to pick up not just pictures, but also floor plans. Open houses show what logs look like in the context of a finished, furnished home, which is what most people actually aspire to live in. Open houses and sales models are great for showing room relationships, proportions and window and lighting placement.

"We modified the company's floor plan to fit the contour and slope of our land, which meant turning the two-story design into three stories to create a walkout basement that didn't feel like a dungeon."

Miller Family
Wheeler Lake, Wisconsin

As you compile your stock of images, don't expect to spot pictures of the exact home you want. Your home hasn't been built yet. Your home will bring together ideas from the photos you see. So learn to look for details within the bigger picture. You may come across a picture of a home that you don't particularly care for, but some element in the home may stand out. Maybe it's some structural component having to do with the logs themselves, or doors, windows, flooring or a fireplace or the kind of stone used in a fireplace. It might just as well be a decorative element, such as furniture, lighting fixtures or even the way a room is arranged.

Recognizing features you like, wherever you find them, will expand your repertoire of ideas and help you define and refine your preferences. It can be an exciting moment when you're leafing through a magazine and spot a picture that makes you say, "This will be perfect for my log home."

Finding Floor Plans

Finding floor plans isn't a problem. There is no shortage. Because home plans are so popular, you'll find plenty in the log-home magazines, on the magazine web sites and in log-home company plans books and on their web sites. You might also find ones that work for you in the many magazines and books that feature floor plans for ordinary houses. Take good ideas wherever you find them. You can even buy cheap software and design your own, not the log part but at least room layouts showing relative size and relationships.

The challenge is finding a plan you know is right for you. This search can be exhausting. There are so many. It may help for you to know that all the log-home floor plans in existence boil down to a handful of themes; the rest are variations. The smaller the home, the fewer the variations.

Many log-home plan sites are searchable by square footage, usually a range of a few hundred square feet. When you're gathering ideas, however, don't limit your possibilities by looking at specific-size plans. Concentrate on generalities.

Look for plans to familiarize yourself with log-home layout conventions: the open layouts, lack of hallways, great rooms, master suites, access to decks. Notice where rooms are in relation to each other, where the stairs and fireplaces are, and how second-level loft areas are configured. Try to spot any layout innovations that might solve your space problem.

You'll miss a lot of these ideas if you survey only plans for the size home you think you want. You may believe you already know the exact size you want your log home to be, but as you move through the process, you might find your goal is a bigger or smaller home, in which case you'll have to go back to square one and search through a new set of plans.

A more beneficial approach is to determine your living needs and how you like your living space arranged. For instance, do you want all the bedrooms in one area, or would you rather have a master bedroom on one side of the house and the children's rooms on the other? Having infrequent overnight company might suggest putting your guest room over a detached garage. If you have an open great room, perhaps a finished basement would be the ideal place for a media room to trap the sound. Think in terms of spatial relationships and flow rather than square footage.

Even before you start looking through plans, make a list of all the features you want and a general layout scheme. Then look at plans that apportion space similarly. You may spot a plan for a 4,800-square-foot house that has everything the way you like it, only there's a huge great room with

> "We knew for certain we wanted to use very large logs, in the vicinity of 12 to 14 inches in diameter and even up to 20 inches. Our designer cautioned us that building a small cabin with that size log would look funny. So we started increasing the square footage to accommodate the logs."
>
> Schmidt Family
> Wilson, Wyoming

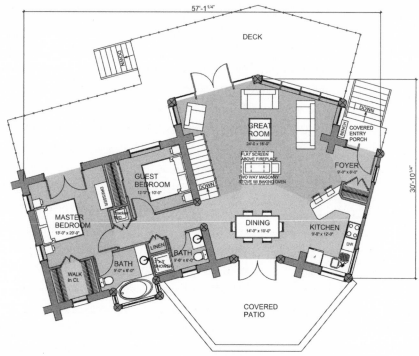

57'-1 1/4"

DECK

DOWN

GREAT
ROOM
24'-0 x 16'-0"

FLAT SCREEN
ABOVE FIREPLACE

TWO WAY MASONRY
STOVE W/ BAKING OVEN

DOWN

COVERED
ENTRY
PORCH

BENCH

FOYER
9'-0" x 6'-0"

GUEST
BEDROOM
12'-0" x 10'-0"

DRESSER

DOWN

30'-10 1/4"

MASTER
BEDROOM
13'-0" x 20'-0"

DINING
14'-0" x 10'-0"

KITCHEN
9'-0" x 12'-0"

DW

LINEN

BATH
9'-0" x 6'-0"

WALK
in CL

BATH
9'-0" x 8'-0"

SHOWER

COVERED
PATIO

FIRST FLOOR PLAN
AREA: 1299 SQ.FT.

LOG HOME DESIGN BY R.C.M. CAD DESIGN DRAFTING LTD.
www.loghomedesign.ca

a sunroom and home office that you definitely don't want. If you delete them from the picture, the result may be 3,600 square feet laid out just the way you want. Shrink everything proportionately to 3,000 square feet, and you're in your budget ballpark. Similarly, small plans often offer ingenious space solutions that you may find appropriate for laying out a portion of your home, such as a cozy conversation nook in a bigger living room.

Once you have a rough idea what you're looking for, then start searching for refinements. The plans you choose don't even have to be from companies you're considering to buy your log home from.

The biggest caveat about floor plans is copyright infringement. This is less a concern with the layout as the overall look of the house that usually accompanies such plans. When people say floor plan, they usually mean the total design. Designs are copyrighted, and companies are becoming increasingly zealous in their pursuit of violators. It is within the realm of possibility that if your home violates a company's design copyright and the litigants are unable to arrive at an acceptable solution, a judge could order you to tear down your house.

"Our open floor plan (the great room, kitchen and second-story loft) makes for easy heating and cooling, but I underestimated how noise carries, especially when my husband raids the fridge in the middle of the night."

Ewing Family
Masonville, Colorado

You have two ways to protect yourself. First, buy the plans. You can hire an architect or even get log-home companies to design a home specifically for you. They'll charge, of course, but then you'll own the plans. You can then use the plans to shop for bids from log-home companies and builders.

The second course of action is to discuss your plans with words, not pictures, at least not while establishing the overall look of the home. If you tell a designer you want the kitchen to be the hub of your great room so it looks out at the entry, dining area and living room, two big turrets flanking the entry, lots of windows to let in light and a master bedroom that has a private porch, you haven't specified any look. You can use your photos to guide interior details after the overall scheme is established. No one has a copyright on furniture arrangement. ❁

Decide on the Look

7

People offer many reasons for wanting a log home. Maybe they like the connection to American history, or they spent time in a family cabin when they were growing up. Perhaps they stayed in a log lodge during a romantic getaway. There are many reasons, few of them practical, all of them valid. But when you pin them down, the reason most everyone gives for wanting a log home is this: "I like the way they look!"

The look of a log home is distinctive. If you looked at a hundred homes and only one was log, you'd recognize it immediately. Yet not all log homes look alike. You'll realize that the moment you begin gathering ideas. While you're sorting through your picture files of the different log-home styles you've seen, some features will stand out, others won't. Don't just ask yourself which log home or homes you prefer; also try to identify what specific features about their look most appeal to you.

You'll gather your ideas individually from many sources, but you'll want to incorporate these favorite features as you try to assemble a coherent image of your ideal home in your mind. These features may be subtle or obvious, but recognizing them and being able to name them will go a long way toward ensuring that you include them in your final design.

The biggest distinctions are log styles (round or square logs, milled or handcrafted), corner styles, chinking or not, and trusses.

Log Styles

Handcrafted logs can be peeled to resemble the tree or hewn to give a flat, finished appearance. Milled logs are shaped with precision machinery. The logs have a uniformity that implies a tight fit and often creates a pleasing visual rhythm.

But logs can be milled to produce a handcrafted look. Some companies hire workers who rough up the machined-smooth surface so it looks like the log was shaped by hand. There are even milling machines that can do the job. So it is possible to get a handcrafted look for a milled-log price. Again, the resulting look matters more than how it is achieved.

Certain log shapes are associated with different regions. The squared log is a tradition of the Appalachian Mountains. Out West, big round logs rule. A popular newcomer is the D-style, which is milled round on the outside and flat on the inside.

Overlapping coped logs without chinking.

Log sizes, measured as diameter or height, vary from about 5 inches to nearly 24 inches. Most milled logs fall within 6 to 10 inches. Hand-peeled or hand-hewn logs start at around 9 inches. Hand-peeled logs have some taper to them, so they might be 10 inches at the top and 15 inches at the bottom, or butt end. Builders compensate for the taper by stacking the logs so that ends and butts alternate and, if calculations are correct, each wall winds up not only level, but also the same height.

Square logs with wide chinking.

Popular Log Profiles

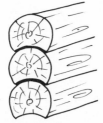

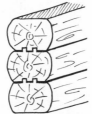

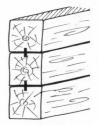

Full-round logs are often connected with splines and require chinking to seal between them.

Swedish cope logs are popular for handcrafted homes. The overlapping helps shed water.

Round-and-round logs are milled flat on the unexposed top and bottom and connected with tongue-and-groove joinery.

D-style milled logs provide a flat interior surface and round exterior, and employ tongue-and groove joinery.

Square logs are connected by splines and use chinking when corner-supported or for decoration.

Run of the Mill

Everyone familiar with log homes knows there are two kinds: handcrafted and milled. Each log-making method has its boosters.

Some extol milled logs as a refinement of handcrafted logs, especially admirers of efficiency and economy. Instead of cutting and shaping tree trunks with axes, adzes, drawknives and chain saws, milled-log producers load the raw material onto a conveyer belt and let rapidly rotating knives do the work. The result is smooth, uniform logs that fit together precisely.

What by hand takes weeks, machines achieve in a day. Talk about your sliced bread.

Widespread mechanization of log making has misled some chroniclers, who attribute the log-home boom that started in the 1970s to the appearance of milled logs. Greater production capacity satisfies rising demand. Makes sense.

Except it isn't true. Milled logs aren't new. They date to the settlement of the English colonies. As Pulitzer Prize-winning author Laurel Thatcher Ulrich declares: "Sawmills were the engine of colonial expansion." Her

book, *The Age of Homespun: Objects and Stories in the Creation of an American Myth,* cites a 1660 map picturing "fifteen sawmills on the streams emptying into New Hampshire's Great Bay."

Surviving to this day is a log home built sometime before 1695 on a point of the bay. Known as the William Damm Garrison, "it was made," Ulrich reports, "of massive timbers squared in a water-powered sawmill until they lay one atop the other like quarried stone." The garrison, built for defense against the native Abenaki, has been moved to Dover and serves as a museum of early colonial life. Other log buildings, which haven't survived, were built in the region, also using milled logs.

On the frontier, sawmills were scarce, so settlers relied on hand tools to fashion logs. Once civilization caught up with them, however, homeowners eagerly clad their rough-hewn logs with milled weatherboards.

Farther west, even in the 19th century, portable sawmills served ranchers. Powered by steam, they were set up at the edge of forests and the base of tree-dense mountains. Loggers cut down trees and dragged them to the sawmills, which turned them into milled lumber and rustic siding.

Milled lumber is a far cry from pre-cut logs. With pre-cut logs, refinements such as notches are added (like Lincoln Log toy building blocks), so that the logs interlock as they are stacked to form walls. No one else having stepped forward to take credit for this advancement, the honor goes to Bruce Ward.

Ward was a long-ago lumberman in northern Maine who supplied northern white cedar logs for utility poles. He used some of the logs to build himself a small cabin on a lake. It was crude, but his friends and neighbors liked its looks. Some asked Ward to build them log cabins. He obliged but realized that if he could standardize the process, he could build more cabins quicker and easier.

In 1923, Ward set up a small mill in Presque Isle, known as the Ward Cabin Company. He assembled his first milled-log cabins at the plant, then took them apart and shipped them to the buyer's site to be reassembled. The cabins lacked the precision milling and sophisticated joinery that make today's well-engineered log homes possible. But they were popular as fishing and hunting camps and vacation cabins, and the company sold them steadily for many years.

As Ward refined the process and expanded his market, he eventually moved the company south to Houlton, which is the last stop on I-95. It's still doing business, as Ward Cedar Log Homes.

Bruce Ward was the great emancipator of log homes. Without him, or the 300 years of American log-milling tradition, folks clamoring for log homes in the 1970s would've had a long wait for the guys with axes, adzes, drawknives and chain saws. It'd be like the Industrial Revolution never happened. 🏵

Corners

Corners are a signature feature of log homes. They provide a measure of structural support but are a major aesthetic consideration of a log home. Basic corner categories are intersecting, overlapping and interlocking.

The most common intersecting corners are butt-and-pass, where one log meets another, which extends beyond it. The logs butt and pass in alternating levels. Butt-and-pass corners are popular with milled-log homes.

Overlapping corners include the cope, or saddle-notch. The carved notch in one log fits over the log below it. If both logs are notched, they fit together like a toy building set.

The most familiar interlocking corner is the dove-tail, which features wedges that are designed to fit tighter as the logs settle into place. The two logs that

Dovetail corners.

form the corner are notched in a modified fan shape, or V, that creates the wedge. Dovetail corners are almost always found with square logs.

Another system, the corner post, uses vertical posts that are slotted, or mortised. The logs feature a tenon, or tongue, at the end that fits into the mortised post. This arrangement gives a finished corner look and allows the logs to slide down the slot as they settle.

Scarf notches are often used with large logs in handcrafted homes.

Chinking

Believe it or not, the biggest bone of contention is chinking, which has plenty to do with the look but little to do with the logs. Chinking originated in log homes where the logs were supported only at the corners, leaving gaps between their horizontal surfaces. Homeowners filled these gaps with mud, manure, horsehair, straw—basically any material they could find to plug the space, even mortar. All these materials were unsatisfactory because they had to be replaced often, but they defined the look of the American frontier cabin.

As log homes gained popularity in the late 1970s, companies that made sealants worked to develop chinking materials that had adhesion and elasticity. Today's products are highly successful in accommodating log movement and exposure to weather, even though in many cases chinking is added purely for looks.

Exterior chinking of corner ends.

Butt-and-pass corners.

Cutting Corners

Corners define the look of log homes and signify solid wood. But corners go beyond appearance and authenticity. For one thing, they solve what to do with the ends of logs. When ordinary walls get to an intersection, builders simply turn and start nailing the lumber in the new direction. Logs stack on their sides. You can cut them to length, but you can't bend them.

Originally, corners' job was to hold log homes up. Logs were stacked rectangularly. When they reached the turning point, their intersection supported the logs vertically. The unbendable ends just stuck out randomly. Although tree trunks are bigger at one end than the other, these walls didn't slant up like an M.C. Escher print because builders alternated large and small ends (more precisely, butts and tapers) so everything turned out level.

Having solved the fitting-together problem, folks turned their attention to those sticking-out log ends. First, they evened them up. Then they aligned the points of contact to support the home and keep things square.

Others took it from there. They developed stronger, more intricate corners. The dovetail, for instance, locks together like a Chinese finger trap. Saddle-notch corners connect powerfully. Scribers and sawmillers soon figured out how to use logs' entire horizontal surface to make contact and provide support. What's more, nowadays everyone relies on fastening devices to keep walls tight as the logs compress and shrink. Even though fasteners technically don't support the wall logs, it's interesting that they go at the corners, through holes drilled or hammered into the wood. Plus, by holding the logs together, corner fasteners do offer some support, albeit in the opposite direction. Corners, meanwhile, have gone from soloist to the chorus.

It's their looks that matter, but even though people declare that looks are the number-one reason they buy log homes, many don't or won't pay enough attention to their corners—not until they open up their log-home company's catalog and see six or more different kinds offered. Now, any company that makes six or more different corners obviously knows corners are a big deal. What's more, choice must be important, too, because if one corner were the best, who would choose another, and what company would be foolhardy enough to even offer others?

So which corner should you choose? Exactly!

Cutting a saddle notch.

Handcrafters often specialize in one corner style, but milled logs can take many shapes. Precision-cut corners appeal especially to home owners descended from nitpickers who considered sticking-out log ends untidy.

Traditionalists in the log-home community cling to the notion of the notch. Notch is what they call hand-made corners. Notching interests them because when you look at the big logs that have to be cut to shape by back-breaking labor, the reward must come after all that peeling and hewing when you get to the end and can unpent your talent for corners.

One log builder who feels passionately about notches is B. Allan Mackie. Through his building, his teaching and his writing, Mackie has influenced at least two generations of log builders. His book *Notches of All Kinds* defines "notch" as "recess near end of a log cut to accept the next log at right angle." Succinct, yet brimming with implication. It speaks volumes, for example, that Mackie regards corner notching as a form of timber joinery, up alongside fashionable mortise-and-tenon.

Hand-gouging a corner notch, every log crafters' mark of skill.

The eloquence of corners lies not in words about them, however. It comes from the image. By announcing the special nature of log homes, corners constitute a big part of the picture. ⚛

Trust the Truss

Sky-high ceilings symbolize today's log homes. Many of these cathedral-like interiors feature trusses. A truss is a rigid framework of beams for supporting a roof. Basically it is a triangle, which everyone recalls from high school is the strongest geometric shape.

The members that make up the truss work in conjunction with one another to resist vertical or "bending-type" loads. The big difference between a truss and a simple beam is that a beam is under compression,

Stonework and log trusses help define the log-home look.

tension and shear simultaneously, while truss members are under compression or tension. Only the connections between the truss members carry shear forces.

How do trusses work in log homes? According to Alex Charvat, a professional engineer specializing in log-home engineering and consulting, "trusses are often used to lessen the spans of ridge beams and purlins. Trees only grow so large and, therefore, there are size limitations on ridge beam dimensions and capacities. The truss becomes an intermediate support for the ridge beam. It is also possible to use a column as an intermediate support, but design requirements may not allow a column to be placed in certain locations, like in the middle of a great room. Basically, the exact designs of structural trusses in a log home are a matter of engineer's preference and the building's architectural requirements."

Of course, in log homes, trusses provide more than support. They also contribute to the look of these homes. That's because cathedral ceilings are open, exposing any trusses that support the roof. The log beams fill the overhead volume and accentuate a ceiling's skywardness. The ideal truss involves almost as much artistry as engineering. Trusses don't have to be decorative, but nothing adds drama to the ceiling of a log-home great room more than a big-log truss.

Trusses have different configurations, depending on their role. Probably the most common truss in log building is the king-post truss, so called because a single post (the king) bisects the basic triangle. A queen-post truss has two posts. The Pratt truss, often used in bridge design, features parallel top and bottom beams, or chords, supported vertically by posts and diagonal braces resembling the letter N.

Back when log-home ceilings were lower, well before the airplane, the most common use for trusses in the United States was building bridges. They featured big timbers, including logs. They had to be engineered to support not only the weight of the wood, but also anything crossing the span, which in bridge-building's heyday was heavy steam locomotives.

A leading civil engineer of this era was Octave Chanute, who designed and built bridges and knew all about trusses. Chanute was also a visionary who believed that human flight was possible. He applied his vision and engineering knowledge to devising a flying machine. He was not alone, but most designs before his imitated the flapping wings of birds and bats. Chanute, according to aviation historian Richard P. Hallion, "established a small flight-testing encampment on the shores of Lake Michigan near Miller, Indiana, in the summer of 1896. Too old to fly himself, he assembled a team of 'test pilots' to evaluate a variety of glider designs. In collaboration with

Augustus Herring, he developed a triplane (three-wing) glider (later modified as a biplane) that had a simple Pratt truss design layout, with evenly spaced ribs, spars, and supporting struts and cross-bracing wires."

Chanute's experiments influenced Orville and Wilbur Wright. Their Flyer, which flew on December 17, 1903, used a modified Pratt truss bracing system to support the upper and lower wings. In other words, trusses helped lift the Wrights off the ground.

Trusses in log homes also create lift, at least a sense of it. They keep the roof off the ground. They also point the spirit heavenward.

Icing on the Cake: Your Roof

People say they want a log home to put a roof over their heads, but they never build the roof out of logs, just the walls. So what type of roof goes with a log home?

Some folks insist that metal is the quintessential log-home roof. Others disagree. Likely as not, people's views are based on what's familiar to them. Tour the urbs and burbs, and the only exterior metal you're likely to see is well-worn 1950s aluminum siding. Today's siding is probably vinyl. Roofs are mostly asphalt shingles.

Metal roofs are outlying. Country churches, farmhouses, barns and outbuildings likely sport metal roofs.

Since log homes are built beyond settlements, you'd expect most would have tin toppings. They don't. People's resistance may stem from their observation that metal roofs rust. But most of the buildings with rusted metal roofs are dilapidated outbuildings. Few farmers spend time or money painting barn roofs.

Actual homes tend to have rust-free roofs. And any on a log home are a charming complement to log walls.

Metal roofs have other, practical benefits. Foremost are their low-maintenance coatings. Primer is baked onto coils of metal, creating a durable base coating. The finish paint coating is applied to the top and bottom of the coil first by roller, then baked on. Coatings are formulated to resist fading, shed dirt and block the growth of algae or fungi, including mildew. And prevent rust.

They're durable. Metal roofs offer a high strength-to-weight ratio and will not lose impact resistance with age. Besides resisting cracking, shrinking and eroding, metal roofs can withstand extreme weather conditions, including hurricanes, tornadoes, hailstorms and severe cold from roof ice dams.

Metal roofs shed snow effectively, making them popular in regions with heavy snow loads. They're also non-combustible, an excellent trait in areas subject to wildfires.

Energy efficiency is another plus. Light colored metal roofs reflect sunlight, keeping the home cooler, but even a dark, shingle-profile aluminum roof rejects 80 to 90 percent of the sun's heat.

A metal roof classes up a log home's act.

As for looks, most people acquainted with metal roofs know about standing seams, which give these roofs the familiar vertical panel look. But today's metal roofs also come in styles that mimic shakes, shingles, slate and tile, and in a wide range of colors.

The metals commonly used in roofing are steel, aluminum, copper, zinc, stainless steel and titanium. Many of the metals have recycled content, varying from 25 percent to 95 percent. Metal roofs cost more than shingles, but most manufacturers guarantee they'll last at least two and a half times longer.

The question most people have about metal roofing is where to buy it. Predictably, there's an organization, called the Metal Roofing Alliance, which has a website that, besides telling you how fantastic metal roofs are, can direct you to contractors in your area that sell and install them. Go to *www.metalroofing.com*.

Before taking that step, however, if you think you might be inclined to put the pedal to the metal, take a closer look at existing log homes that have tin roofs. Roofs constitute a big part of the look of particular homes,

Good log-home design apportions volume proportionately, from the square footage to the roof.

just like log styles, corners, chinking and other design features that are a matter of preference. Make sure a metal roof is something you want to live with because it'll last a long time, longer even than your mortgage.

Subtler Distinctions

There are subtler distinctions that you'll become aware of as you gather more ideas. The important thing is to recognize what draws you to these homes.

Perhaps the attraction of a log home has little to do with the actual logs. That sounds silly at first, but the characteristics that people associate with log homes can easily apply to other homes: living in the country, the great room with cathedral ceilings, open flow. So, even though the look is why most people want a log home, there's more to living in a log home than the looks of the home.

Imagine the look you love in a setting that enhances or completes the look. Some people who build among trees like their log home to echo the trees in some way, such as color or size. Maybe your land has cedar trees growing on it, so you want cedar logs. Maybe you want a green roof to suggest the leaves of trees. Or green trim around the doors and windows to continue the leafy theme. Or red to contrast with the green.

You have so many opportunities to determine the look of your house to express your idea of what a log home should be. Learn about as many options as you can to make the choice that you decide is right for you. ✿

Logs add character to homes that transcends their structural role.

Calculate How Much House You Can Afford

8

If all goes smoothly, sooner or later you'll find yourself at the turning point where dream confronts reality. This can be an anxious moment, mainly because from this point on, you'll need money. Lots of it.

Too many people are misled as to what a log home costs. You can blame it on the way they're sold. You browse a company's catalog of homes and spot an appealing model called the Prairie Classic. You call up the log-home company and ask how much the Prairie Classic will cost and are told $85,000 plus shipping, not counting the cost of the land. Perhaps you already own your land, and you've been around the block enough times to know there'll be a few incidental extras that drive up that $85,000 figure. But that's the number sticking in your mind. It is going to be a rude awakening when you find out that $85,000 Prairie Classic home is going to wind up costing, when all is said and done, $524,000.

But all you can muster is $346,000. And your heart is set on moving into that Prairie Classic. Face it, your expectation is going to ensure that just about any other home will be a letdown.

What if you approached the situation from the opposite direction? You tell a log-home company you own your land and are looking for a home in the $300,000 range. The sales rep, who has sold maybe 30 homes over the years and has a pretty good idea what they wind up costing, opens the company plan book and recommends three models. You look at them and like the looks of the Loon Lake Lodge model. The rep tells you that ought to wind up costing you around $290,000, and the company will sell you the logs and plans for that model for $63,900. You're excited for two reasons: You like the house, and the cost is well within your budget.

Now, not later, is the time to find out not how much you'll need, but how much you have. Your cash on hand (savings plus equity) plus the amount you can or want to borrow equals your budget. You cannot exceed this sum. How much of it you're willing to spend on your log home is your decision. Economic uncertainty may suggest caution, or you may throw caution to the wind and blow your whole wad.

If you're counting on borrowing money, however, you need to understand how that works. Two principles that you may be unfamiliar with are construction financing and comparables.

"We wanted a bigger master bedroom, so we added a wing, then balanced that with another wing, where we put the dining room so it wouldn't take any space away from our living room."

Pugh Family
Western North Carolina

You'll probably need a conventional mortgage loan after the home is built. It will be based on the predicted market value of the home. Before that, you'll need a construction loan to pay for your log package and for the labor and other materials to assemble your home.

Construction loans aren't outside most lenders' experience, but what makes them different for a log home is that the log package usually must be paid for at the time of delivery. This is a substantial cost that front-loads the cash disbursement, or draw, rather than staggering it more or less evenly at regular intervals.

Your lender will arrange a draw schedule during construction to pay your builder and any others at regular intervals until the home is completed. During construction, you'll repay only the interest on the loan. When the home is done, the loan balance will roll over into the mortgage.

The mortgage amount will be based on the appraised future value of the home. The appraiser, who is hired by the lender, determines the value by comparing it to similar homes in the immediate area. Appraisers for

lenders considering a log-home mortgage usually have trouble finding comparable homes because log homes are rarely built in well laid-out neighborhoods with other log homes. In addition, the value of comparables is determined by the price of recently sold similar homes. Log-home owners tend to live in their homes longer than people live in ordinary homes, so appraisers often have trouble determining a fair-market value for a log home built in a relatively isolated setting.

A good appraiser can work out a formula to arrive at a reasonable value for your home, often by relying on the cost per square foot to build other custom homes in the area where your log home will be built. To confound appraisers even more, however, log-home owners tend to overbuild for these areas, not just by building larger homes than the average, but also by using higher-grade materials and furnishings, which add cost to the construction of a home but don't necessarily increase its market value. If your project will cost $350 a square foot and other custom homes have been averaging $250, you'll raise a red flag with the appraiser. Basically, anything that deviates from the norm could pose a problem.

That right there is the reason many lenders won't even consider financing a log home. They don't know how much to lend because they don't know how much they'll be able to get for the home if they're stuck

having to foreclose. Based on recent experiences in the mortgage market, where banks got greedy and made bad loans and got burned and wound up owning homes that they themselves overvalued, you can understand how, now that they've sobered up from their binge, they're looking to avoid anything that smacks of risk.

It's unlikely that the bank that holds the mortgage on your existing home will leap at the opportunity to lend you loads of money to buy your log home, even if your credit score is 800. Risk is a factor but less an issue than unfamiliarity with the undertaking.

Short of having so much cash that you don't need to borrow any, there are two possible solutions:

Find a lender where you intend to build your log home, if there are other log homes in the area, especially if they are log homes made by the same company you're buying yours from. These lenders will understand the process and be familiar with the eccentricities of log-home buying and building.

Talk to a lender that specializes in log-home financing. Any log-home company you're talking to ought to be able to suggest several such lenders that have financed purchases of their homes. If not, just Google "log home lenders."

Since most people need financing (and I don't know of a log-home company that offers it), you'll likely be dealing with a lender for both your construction and mortgage loans. Again, sooner is better than later to find out where you stand. Pre-qualifying can provide an estimate of the amount you can borrow so you can calculate your budget.

Pre-qualification establishes how much you intend to borrow and whether you can repay it. The process starts with your telling your loan officer how much money you make and how much you owe. Usually this is a verbal step, with no formal application yet. It helps to have your lender look at your credit report.

After you settle on the purchase of your log package and arrange for the home's construction, you'll make a formal application for mortgage

"Originally, we planned for a very large master bedroom suite, only to realize this would add greatly to the cost. We had to ask ourselves, where do we want to spend our time? We knew we didn't need as much space for sleeping as we did for being with our family, so we scaled back on the bedroom for extra space in the common areas."

Casebolt Family
Steamboat Springs, Colorado

approval. Assuming that you survive the appraisal process, your lender will arrange a draw schedule prior to construction and then make payments according to the schedule.

You may have to modify the draw schedule and amounts, depending on changes to the project or unexpected expenses, but having gotten the ball rolling, that's a punch you can roll with. Considering where you are in the process at this moment, actual money matters probably lie well off in the future and certainly won't occur before you have made a lot of decisions as to the specific home you'll be buying and building. But by being aware of the entire financing process and preparing for it, you won't find yourself overly frustrated or even thwarted when the time comes to show the money. ✿

Know When and How to Compromise 9

After you determine how much money you can and want to spend, don't hesitate to share that figure with any log-home company you're considering. Knowing your budget will help the company show you what's available in your price range. You may be disappointed, but you might also be pleasantly surprised to find out what you can afford. Either way, it's better to face reality sooner than later.

If you see right off the bat that the discrepancy between dream and reality is great, don't despair. Adjust your expectations.

The most obvious step is to simplify your design. Fewer corners equals lower cost, and it's cheaper to build up or down than out. Or you can reduce the size of your house. Most people don't believe they can make do with less space, but you'd be surprised. The difference between 3,500 square feet and 3,000 isn't that great, but the cost savings might make the difference in whether you can afford a log home or have to settle for another kind. Just don't make your dream home so small that you wind up cramping your lifestyle.

If you aren't familiar with the Not-So-Big-House concept, investigate it. It stems from a book by architect Sarah Susanka that has swelled to a movement advocating simplicity and sensibility. The essence of the

Not-So-Big movement isn't downsizing per se but making the most of the space you have. It advocates many space-saving strategies.

Among them is designing rooms to serve double-duty. You may already be applying that principle by using a guest room as a home office during the 45 or so weeks a year that company isn't spending the night. It also works exceedingly well in homes with open layouts, which many log-home owners favor anyway. Here are some other cost compromises that will lower the cost of your home.

Substitute carpeting over subfloor for hardwood floors. You can always install a hardwood floor later, maybe even a higher grade than you initially hoped for.

Instead of a traditional fireplace, install a more efficient stove. It might seem like too much of a compromise, since fireplaces define the log-home look for most people, but when you look at enough pictures, you'll notice that stoves enhance the log-home atmosphere plenty. There are middle grounds, too, including a gas fireplace without the towering, massive stone chimney that not only costs way more than the firebox, but also requires super-duper foundation footings to support the extra weight. A more modest surround with a gas insert has a homey look that cozies up a room and doesn't cost a fortune to fuel.

If you can afford the upfront cost of the big old fireplace, but aren't

A high-efficiency wood-burning fireplace has blowers to circulate the heat and a large glass door for viewing the cozy fire.

looking forward to wasting money on looks but little heat, consider a high-efficiency fireplace insert for your beautiful fireplace. Or even a masonry stove which relies on the thermal mass of brick and stone to soak up the heat and then release it slowly. All these alternatives will more than return your investment as the years go by.

Use stock rather than custom, particularly for kitchen and bathroom cabinets. Some of the finest cabinetmakers offer lower-price lines that are indistinguishable in quality from their top-of-the-line products. The difference might be as minor as fewer door choices or finish options.

You can later upgrade many fixtures and appliances. Or you can add items—just plan for them

Log walls mixed with drywall add variety and lightness.

so there is wiring and plumbing and adequate space as needed. Yes, that includes the hot tub. Don't go overboard, however, and, above all, avoid builder-grade anything. (Builder grade is the lowest level of quality and exists primarily to allow builders to submit lowball bids.)

You may be savvy enough to buy some components you want for your log home yourself. We haven't discussed log-home kits yet, but, not to give anything away, these kits come in varying degrees of completion. Most people prefer the kit and caboodle, but most of the caboodle is materials you can buy yourself. You can even bypass your local lumber store. All kinds of quality vintage furnishings and fixtures, including solid-wood doors and double-hung windows turn up at architectural salvage yards and Habitat for Humanity's ReStore. Plenty of brand-new fixtures and materials are available online. Again, let your computer mouse do the clicking.

Use pine logs instead of a costlier species. The wood you use doesn't matter structurally. All wood, even that purported to be naturally decay resistant, needs to be protected with a wood preservative. Properly maintained, pine can last as long as any other wood. And some people actually prefer the look of pine.

You can also mix full log and framed construction. In fact, this mix is common even in expensive log homes. You may not realize that most two-story log homes are full log only on the first level. The second floor may be framed and use a complementary exterior material, such as board-and-batten, barn wood or even log siding milled by your log-home company to match the wood species and look of your full-log walls. Inside the home, partition walls can be framed and drywalled. Many people actually prefer some drywall, even on the main level, especially in bathrooms, bedrooms and sometimes even kitchens. Drywall is a great compromise for families that want some but not all log interiors. Plumbers and electricians appreciate drywall, too, because it doesn't require the planning that logs do for pipes and wires.

Ask your log-home company for cost-saving suggestions. For example, the company could easily modify (simplify) the plan you like or show you a more affordable plan that retains the same layout features as your first choice. The company, or perhaps even an architect or a log builder, might apply some imagination and come up with an overall look that doesn't cram your log home into a basic box.

The ultimate compromise, of course, is that you can postpone building until you have saved or can borrow more.

Meanwhile, maybe your decision will be easier if you re-examine what you're looking for in a log home. An earlier chapter (*Decide on the Look*) discussed the various log styles and features that define log homes. The point was for you to become aware of them to identify those elements that best represent your idea of what a log home should look like and then

> "We chose a small wood-burning stove to heat the great room because a big stone hearth would just hide too many wall logs. The stove is extremely functional and economical."
>
> Grzybowski Family
> Wyoming

proceed to design and build a home that embodies those features. So, now you realize that owning a log home featuring the look you want is beyond your means. You aren't the first person to face this predicament.

Occasionally, people think they want a log home when what they really want is a home that looks like a log home. Some people don't even want that; they just want a sense of logs.

The point is that log homes aren't right for everyone. Even if they were easy to buy and build, many people would shy away from them. At some critical point, preferably sooner than later, you'll have discovered enough about log homes to make the go or no-go decision. Pilots refer to the point of no return, where they either turn back if the going gets tough or commit to proceed to their destination. When you reach your point of no return, you are committing to completing the project or abandoning it. This is that point.

Regardless of whether you decide go or no-go, identify those aspects of a log-home look that really matter to you and investigate whether you can achieve them without going the whole log-home route. Here are some alternatives to full-log construction.

Half-Logs

This style of log home began as a way to increase energy efficiency in northern climates. The principle is to build a conventional wall with insulation, then create a super-insulated sandwich by applying split logs to the inside and outside of the wall. I stress split logs rather than log siding, so that you wind up with a wall containing the full log, only in two parts, rather than a less sturdy and less durable veneer of log siding. From the standpoint of looks, few people can tell the difference between a half-log and a full-log wall. The look-alikeness is what increased their popularity among people who shied away from log construction but favored the log look.

Half-log homes became popular outside the north for their looks, ease of construction for non-log builders and for their insulation, which turns out to be as effective in super-hot climates as in super-cold.

Half logs for the walls with log corner posts and chinking.

Half-log companies have broadened their log styles. You can even find hand-crafted half-logs. At the other extreme, it's possible to mill the exterior half in a clapboard or some other conventional siding configuration so that the home will fit in communities where full-log homes might look out of place or actually be banned by your homeowners association or architectural review board. Then you can order the interior half-log as rustic looking as you like, even applying chinking between logs to get an old-timey cabin look.

Log Siding

This is always a money-saving option, and good value for second stories and even lower levels where full logs would add cost or represent a maintenance issue. But cladding an entire house with log siding may be expecting too much. Its best application might be on a log element house that has lots of exterior stone and glass and some other wood, such as shingles or board-and-batten, where the log siding can be applied more strategically to highlight smaller spots, perhaps even a fancier siding with a chinking groove.

Log Elements

Some people like logs but only a little. You may define a log home as having an open great room with big log trusses, a log-beam ceiling in the kitchen and master bedroom, log railings, maybe log posts supporting a loft. Sometimes logs that contribute to the look of a log home not only have nothing to do with its being a log home, but don't even function structurally. These elements are easily incorporated into a non-log home. In fact, in the past 10 years as log homes have soared in popularity, many homeowners initially drawn to log homes have settled for log elements or accents, not for money reasons but to achieve a look they love that isn't too loggy.

Log accents convey suggestions of the log look.

Log accents are popular in mountain homes and other homes with rustic styling. They also add distinctive touches to conventional homes that incorporate a lot of stone and glass.

You buy log accents from a log producer. Some producers look disdainfully at customers who don't want to buy a log home, but that's their problem, not yours. When you show up to order some heavy timber trusses, big log posts and a few other log elements, most producers are not only happy for the business, but also eager to contribute to a home that will have some flair.

Laminated or Engineered Timbers

Created by pressure-adhering dimensional lumber to the thickness of a log and then milling it to a log profile, so-called glue-lams, or glu-lams, have limited application as wall logs, although they work aesthetically when the two outer boards are a better grade of wood, such as cedar over pine. I've seen two lam-log homes, and both owners were satisfied. The logs look authentic enough, except at the corners, where the layered construction is exposed at the log ends. Long-term durability can be problematic if glue-lams are overexposed to harsh sunlight. They work best inside for spanning large open spaces and for trusses, especially with flat-surface wall logs. In these capacities, they're usually cheaper than full logs.

Concrete Logs

Yes, there are such things. They aren't cheap. There have been advances in coloration. They're concrete. One is displayed at the airport in Missoula, Montana, which is practically ground zero for real-log production. You want to live in a bunker, though, import one from pre-free Albania, where Commie boss Enver Hoxha built beaucoup bunkers to fuel national para-noia of imminent invasion by soft-liners. But concrete log homes are way above bunkers, and if you do decide one is right for you, you can warm it up immeasurably by adding some real-log accents.

Knowing you have other options than full-log construction might help you buy a home you can afford that doesn't require you to sacrifice much in the way of looks. In fact, by combining aspects of the log-home look you like with the necessary compromises to fit your budget, you may wind up living in a home that suits you perfectly. ❀

Anticipate the Unexpected 10

Even after you have obtained a contract price for your logs and realistic bids for the rest of the materials and labor involved in building the home, that's no guarantee it'll get built for that amount. Surprises during construction usually involve unanticipated costs. The biggest budget-busters are site preparation and changes to the design after construction begins.

Site Preparation

You're usually dealing with raw, often remote sites. No one is likely to know whether the soil covers underground rock that will require blasting before the foundation can be dug or how deep down water lies for the well you'll need to dig.

Design Changes after Construction Begins

Changes are so common that the term "change order" is part of every builder's lexicon. Some even have pre-printed forms just for changes. Modifications are sometimes necessary, but more often they result from recognizing that things would work out better by deviating from the original plan. You see the log walls for the living room and realize a bigger window would really showcase the drop-dead view. Or you realize you'll be finishing the basement not too far down the road, so why not enclose the furnace and water heater now rather than later?

Taken individually, changes aren't usually all that expensive. But they add up. A few thousand here, a few thousand there, and suddenly you're facing $10,000, maybe $20,000 more than you budgeted—and it was a tight budget to begin with.

Some changes can be avoided by better planning and making sure your written contract with your builder is specific and detailed. A common dispute between contractors and homeowners is their interpretations of contracts. You specify that bathrooms are to have one faucet that controls hot and cold water, but you don't specify the quality of that faucet. The contractor bids the job for a builder-grade faucet. You see it installed and argue that you expected better. It isn't in writing, though.

> "During the construction of our log home, it rained for almost six weeks. All of the logs turned dark. However, much to our surprise, we cleaned them with bleach and water, and they were restored."
>
> Watts Family
> Upper Peninsula, Michigan

BEFORE: Log purlins and ridge beam being set with a crane.

Ultimately, you get the faucet you wanted, but you'll also be paying the builder for the price difference—plus the labor involved in uninstalling the first faucet and any restocking fee the contractor has to pay to return it to the supplier.

You can imagine bigger disputes arising that require mediation and perhaps even legal resolution. These distractions add cost and delay the project, adding more cost. Ultimately, your contractor holds the edge by having the ability to place a lien on your property if you don't pay for the changes, even if you don't regard them as changes.

Upgrades Once the Project is Under Way

Not every added cost results from change orders. Mid-grade appliances are better than suitable for just about any home, but as yours takes shape, you realize you want a better model or a classier brand. Or you see the deck and figure the hot tub you thought you could get by without is now essential.

AFTER: Finished home with stucco on the gable ends and stonework on the foundation and chimney.

The Cost of Utility and Other Hookups

They can increase suddenly and significantly. Water and sewer hookup in the resort where we have our weekend home went up $8,000 overnight. Our neighbors, who had just started building their log cabin, had budgeted at the old rate. They had to postpone their satellite TV dish.

Even the most conservative estimates say to add 10 to 15 percent to your budget for overrun. If it turns out you don't need the money, there isn't a problem. If you do need it, you'll avoid having to borrow more money, inevitably at a higher rate because your original lender may balk at advancing more after the project is under way, requiring you to get a new loan or, worst possible scenario, billing the overrun to your credit card.

In fact, when you calculate your budget, you're better off keeping a cash reserve separate from your budget altogether. Think of everything that can go wrong in your life that is totally unrelated to your log-home project. Abandoning your dream because your car needs a new transmission, your child needs braces or you lose your job is not something you want to happen. The better prepared you are, the likelier you'll be to weather a storm.

Those same neighbors who got hit with the unanticipated water and sewer hookup hike finished their project so far over budget that they had to put off enjoying their second home and turn it into a rental property instead. All their hard work for someone else's enjoyment. And wouldn't you know that the first thing the rental agent told them they'd need to add to help it rent better was a satellite TV dish. ✿

Add 10 to 15 percent to your budget for cost overrun.

Buy Your Land Before You Buy Your House

11

Good design flows from its surroundings. You don't need to be Frank Lloyd Wright to realize that views and natural features of your land (terrain, vegetation, sunlight) will influence the form of your home. View, for example, which some people regard as a requirement for log homes, can affect the number, size and location of windows in your home and the resulting balance of wood and glass. Views might also determine whether you have an expansive deck to gaze out at a majestic vista or a shade porch to sit and watch a dramatic sunrise or sunset.

Slope will be another factor. The hilliness of your site could decide whether you have a walkout basement (which can save your adding a second story), as well as the orientation of the front and back of your house. A steep slope could even determine whether you can build on your property or at the very least whether construction costs will be significantly higher than for a more moderate incline.

As for the specific size and shape of your house, the time to apply those parameters to the design of your home is after you buy your land rather than before. There are folks who design an eye-catching house first, then head out seeking a likely spot to build it. Most, though, buy their land first, then seek inspiration from it. The aim is to arrive at a design that complements the site rather than contradicts it. Of course, you're entitled to plan a general layout anytime, and some people have built lovely homes from plans they drew up long before they located the land. In fact, having a sense of how you prefer to configure your home can actually guide you when you shop for land. But choosing a design first and then sticking with it no matter what could more easily lead to disappointment if it is finally built on an incompatible site.

Almost all log homes are built on rural or remote sites. Before you buy property, get the lay of the land. Some people crave unspoiled solitude, especially those who anticipate retiring soon and envision building their dream home amid the uncluttered outdoors, so scrutinize not just the actual property you're interested in, but also land that is adjacent and in the general vicinity.

How does one go about finding and buying raw land? The task seems especially challenging after hearing that country folk selling land know its value very, very well and invariably come out way ahead in any sale.

Don't let that conventional wisdom discourage you. You can level the playing field with common sense and research.

Start by finding out what land has been selling for in the area you're considering. Transactions are public record. As for locating a specific piece of property, consult a real-estate agent where you're hoping to buy. Also, check the local paper.

Not all land for sale has a for-sale sign. But all land is owned, and all owners are listed on the local tax rolls. If you spy a spot you particularly like, contact the owner and express your interest. More than one homeowner has told of inquiring about the perfect parcel right before the landowner was about to put property on the market.

When you do find land, don't overbuy. People moving to the country often assume 40 to 100 acres are optimum. Unless you intend raising livestock or cash crops, 5 to 10 acres are usually adequate for a home site and surroundings.

Don't subject yourself to unwanted intrusion, however, especially if your land's main attraction is a kick-ass view. A wooded buffer might be worth paying extra for. You may even find a smaller lot adjoining a state forest or park or protected wetlands. Generally, though, be wary of vast tracts of uncleared land around you. Farmland is notoriously susceptible to rampant development, especially the way suburbs keep sprawling. Green pastures today might be townhouse cul-de-sacs tomorrow. Even in the apparent middle of nowhere, you never know what will one day occupy them. If the local municipality has a master plan, check for future highways, annexations and the general trend of development. You could be delighted to learn plans call for an 18-hole golf course practically in your back yard. A rendering plant or windmill farm may evoke less enthusiasm.

Even if the land remains sparsely settled, it's frustrating buying the ideal piece of property and then finding out once you've built your home that your new neighbor is moving his collection of rusted-out school buses

onto his property. Do you have any protection from such eyesores, short of starting a feud? Zoning or covenants in some rural areas can be laissez-faire or even hypothetical. Your nearest municipality or the homeowners' association can tell you what the rules are and whether they are actually enforced.

When you think you've found the right property, consider hiring a real-estate lawyer. A real-estate agent works for the person selling the property, but a real-estate lawyer acts on your behalf, checking out the seller's title, easements, liens and any murky areas that need to be resolved or might cause you problems after the sale. And with undeveloped rural land, there might be plenty. A real-estate lawyer will cost $200 or more an hour, but in two or three hours the person should be able to tell you whether the land you're eyeing is worth buying. Considering what you stand to lose on the deal or in subsequent litigation, the price to pay is small.

"A topographical map of our mountainside lot was a key element in the design of the house. The site is steeply sloped and required a multi-faceted foundation. On the blueprints, I marked each variation with a colored marking pen. It looked like a veritable rainbow when I was finished."

Cecich Family
Western Montana

If the property hasn't been surveyed recently, say within the past 20 to 30 years, consider adding a contingency in the purchase contract that lets you back out without penalty if a survey finds the actual boundaries differ from those represented. This is a common problem in the East, where land records go back centuries and long-ago errors may have gone unnoticed. It's reasonable for land buyers to require the seller to pay for a survey or deduct it from the selling price.

Once you buy land, even before you build, it becomes an asset you can use as collateral to apply toward financing the purchase of your log home. Meanwhile, you can enjoy your land for camping, picnicking, hunting, fishing (if you're fortunate enough to have a stream or pond) or growing vegetables. Or just walking the land seeking inspiration to guide the design of the home you're looking forward to building.

If you might be waiting a year or longer to break ground, take the time to note seasonal changes, not just of vegetation, but also sunlight and shade. This information, too, will prove useful when you plan the location and look of your home.

Finding the right piece of property requires work, but it's the foundation of your home and the lifestyle that your home will represent. And once you're satisfied you've bought the right land for your home in the country, you're ready to take the next step: designing the actual home to suit your land. That's when the fun begins.

Sitting Pretty

Many factors determine the best place to build your log home on your property. If you own a small lot, you probably have little choice. Even on a sprawling parcel, there may be only one obvious location. Usually, however, several possibilities may loom.

Suppose you buy five or more acres atop a hill. Your first inclination might be to build your home on the ridge. Closer scrutiny could reveal greater advantages to building a little lower. Doing so can avoid constant exposure to the elements, especially harsh winter winds. Or your mountain-top panorama may be marred in one direction by unsightly cooling towers from some distant nuclear power plant, wind farm or antenna array.

You may prefer to forgo the 360-degree panorama and focus the view toward a particularly impressive landmark, say a lake or scenic valley, or to gain a dramatic sunrise or sunset. Building into the hillside can also give you a sloping site, which is ideal for a walkout basement that will save you the cost of adding a second story.

Many factors will influence your choice of one particular spot over another. They boil down to two categories: aesthetics and practicality.

Beauty may be in the eye of the beholder, but don't let emotion totally overrule common sense. In other words, there are two sides to every view. The first, of course, is the perspective that will be enjoyed from the house. The second is how the house itself will appear on the landscape. One that fails to harmonize with its setting may afford the owner an inspirational vantage, while, to its neighbors, it sticks out like a sore thumb.

Where aesthetics are concerned, there is one rule to follow: Go with the flow. Regardless of size, wherever you decide to build your house, strive to flatter the land.

Practical considerations are more complicated. They include topographical features, orientation and access. (More about this in the next chapter.)

Terrain presents some aesthetic consequences, but for the most part it involves down-to-earth decisions. Besides the possibility of undesirable exposure from a hilltop location, a valley setting also raises issues. As air cools at night, it moves from higher elevations to lower ones, producing effects that may be desirable or not, depending on your circumstances.

Likewise, a ledge location halfway up a slope that is initially appealing may eventually become precarious. Think California mudslides.

Having a dependable water source available to firefighters could lower insurance premiums.

Then there are windbreaks, whether from the contour of the land itself or from vegetation, particularly trees. Trees also can affect the amount of sunlight that hits the house. Building just north of a stand of deciduous trees, for example, may provide warming sun in the winter and cooling shade in summer. Conifers in the same spot will block the sun year round.

Avoid building too close to large stands of trees. If carelessness or lightning ignites them, well-stoked flames can quickly threaten the house. Although log homes are less susceptible to fire than ordinary houses, in the face of a raging wildfire, all homes are vulnerable.

In remote settings, there is value in having a pond near the house, whether naturally occurring or created. Having a dependable water source available to firefighters could substantially lower insurance costs. Ponds are also pretty to look at, either from the house or an outdoor room.

Nearby bodies of water must certainly be taken into account. Any northerner familiar with the concept of lake-effect snow will understand the wisdom of locating a home away from the path of winter winds whipping across water. At the same time, homes in milder climates may be situated to take advantage of cooling summer breezes blowing in from the water.

Every location has what are known as prevailing winds. That is, the wind generally blows from one direction in the summer and from the opposite direction in winter. This principle explains why airport runways are aligned in certain directions. In fact, the nearest airport is a good place

to inquire about the prevailing winds in your area. Other good sources are your local weather station or state energy office.

Avoid building where topographical features funnel the wind, intensifying its velocity—a phenomenon known as the Venturi effect. Instead, seek areas where the wind speed is constant. If you don't have such a spot, plant trees or build a garage that can block or redirect the wind.

Consider the impact of topography on construction costs. Steep, rocky or densely wooded sites will add time and money to the project.

Steep, rocky
or densely
wooded sites
will add time
and money to
the project.

Once you've explored the terrain and found a likely spot, turn your attention to orientation—which way a house is turned on that spot. Usually the determining factor is sunlight. Most houses are rectangular. To maximize solar gain, align your home east and west so that the long sides face north and south. Wisdom dictates having the entrance face south and fewer windows facing north. When laying out the rooms, place the more frequently used areas on the south side.

You may have good reason for reversing this arrangement, however, especially if you are building just south of a road and don't want your home facing away from it. You may also want a south-facing sunroom in back of the house.

When considering your home's orientation, check the sun's path before deciding where to put windows and skylights. If you are able, track light throughout the year. The farther north you build, the greater the seasonal extremes.

These factors will guide your decision where to build. What's more, they will suggest subsequent landscaping after you move in. Using existing natural features as a starting point will aid in achieving harmony with your setting.

Above all, remember that these are guidelines, not hard-and-fast rules. The best part of building from scratch on your land is being able to do what you decide is best for you. At the same time, heeding conventional wisdom from those who have confronted the same problems, as well as seeing the big picture, will allow you to get the most enjoyment from your home. ✳

Make Sure You Can Build on Your Land

12

When you eventually find the land you love, your first consideration should be whether you can build on it. You can't always. The reasons may be physical or legal.

Because log homes tend to be built in out-of-the-way locations, many homeowners assume they are beyond jurisdictions and that common sense governs their activities. A rude awakening often awaits. Others, apprehensive over the prospect of living in lawless wilderness, seek semi-tamed land. Both circumstances require precautions.

The popularity of second homes has prompted the rise of developed communities. Their appeal is obvious. They provide a planned infrastructure—including roads, water, waste removal, natural gas and electricity—where the cost for individual homeowners might be prohibitive. These resorts also offer essential services, especially security and, where necessary, snowplowing. Many feature amenities, such as on-site recreation, a common meeting place and perhaps even a restaurant.

Some of these mountain, woodland or waterside communities have substantial initiation and recurring membership fees; others are priced well within the reach of average families. In almost all cases, they have lots for sale where you can build your dream home. All you need do is show your plans to the governing homeowners association or architectural review committee. To guide you, there are covenants that clearly or vaguely state the kind of homes that may or cannot be built.

It often comes as a shock to someone who has bought a lot at one of these resort communities and intends to build a beautiful log home that these covenants sometimes declare no rustic-style homes. Perhaps they even come right out and specify no log homes allowed. Could anything be more heartbreaking?

> "We wanted a detached garage, but we found out you can't have two buildings on one building permit, so we had to connect the two and built a carport between them."
>
> Gaura Family
> New Salem, North Carolina

If you're thinking that buying land in a resort community may be the perfect situation for your, the time to find out whether log homes are permitted is before you buy the land and pay the initiation fee. Sometimes these places allow some kinds of log homes but not others. Hoity-toity communities typically shun outright "cabins," for example.

A hindrance outside these self-governing enclaves is federal, state and perhaps even local environmental restrictions, particularly those concerning wetlands. Coincidentally, many rural-land buyers often desire property with access to water. Growing awareness of the ecological significance of the land surrounding water has tightened restrictions.

Restrictions aren't always imposed to protect wildlife or fragile ecosystems. I recall one instance where a couple who owned a 20-year-old log home next to water wanted to build an addition. They had no problem getting a permit to build the original home, but in the intervening years, their land had been designated a hundred-year flood plain. As a consequence, they had to build their addition farther back and higher up than the original house. The result was two separate buildings connected by a sloping breezeway, sort of House and House Junior. If you bought waterfront property several years ago but are only just now thinking about building on it, be sure to get an update on what currently is or isn't allowed.

Curtailments apply to other places than wetlands. The once wide-open West is becoming more law-ridden day by day. In other words, it's catching up with the rest of the country. Anything doesn't always go, so if you're looking to build where it still does, don't dally.

Even land that isn't officially restricted still might not be considered buildable from a practical standpoint. Again, wildfires spring to mind. Your land still must meet several conditions before you can break ground for your dream home.

It must have a suitable building site. You need a relatively flat spot with access for construction equipment. A gentle slope is fine, especially if you want a walkout basement, but a steep hillside poses challenges—and higher building costs. Deep soil that can be easily excavated for a solid foundation is preferable to subsurface rock that requires blasting.

It must have access to water and good drainage. Unless your land is linked to municipal water and sewer systems, you'll need a well and a septic tank and leach field. You also want good drainage to move water

away from your house and avoid flooding. To make sure the land drains, you'll need a percolation test. The local health department can tell you whether your land meets the requirements for a septic field (basically another flat spot).

It should have direct access. If the property isn't on a road, it may need an easement through a neighboring property so you can get to the road. Easements work both ways. Make sure you know whether your land has existing easements allowing neighbors to cross it, especially if you're planning on installing a gate with a lock (which may be prohibited).

If your property is sizable and the only building site is well off the main road, you'll need a driveway. The farther you build from the road, the more driveway you'll have to plow in winter and maintain in all seasons. You may get by without paving it, but you'll at least want crushed stone, roadbase, or recycled asphalt or concrete to cover the mud and grading to smooth out ruts that will develop over time.

"We envisioned a main house with several smaller cabins, but our subdivision restricts owners to just one building, so we designed an 8,000-square-foot cabin, built into a bluff."

Sansom Family
Eastern Utah

You'll surely need a driveway or access of some kind for trucks delivering your logs and any heavy construction equipment involved in preparing your site and erecting the home. The alternatives for getting heavy logs to your site are a helicopter or a forklift to offload all your logs and carry them to the site pretty much one at a time. Both these solutions cost plenty and still don't address day-to-day access for construction crews and for you after the home is built.

Any driveway that crosses water requires a bridge. Bridges that don't wash away or collapse cost plenty, more than you can imagine when the county engineers must give approval.

By the way, don't invest in a really nice driveway until after the home is built and all the construction equipment is done driving to and from the job site.

It needs access to utilities. You may try forgoing a telephone landline, but electricity isn't wireless or digital. The farther you are from existing lines, the more the power company will charge you to hook up. Building new is a good time to think about off-the-grid living, especially solar and wind power, and even geothermal.

Clearing land isn't a requirement for buildability, but the expense can make building prohibitive. Building near trees is cheaper than among them; removing trees costs less before you build than after.

Meeting these conditions might yield a piece of property that you can build the perfect home on. Then again, it may not. You can avoid frustration by being flexible. A great view is desirable, for example, but insisting on one could add time and money to your project.

As crowded as America may seem, plenty of raw land is still available. Some land will not permit or support a dwelling, however. Other land may be prohibitive to develop. Before buying any land you hope to build your log home on, investigate what the future has in store.

Hug Those Trees
The romantic notion of a log home as a cabin in the woods depends on having the woods. Many homeowners prefer to set their new log home

among trees. Some clearing is necessary to build the home and desirable to promote ambient airflow. Too often, however, trees are unnecessarily lost in the construction process. If you value your trees, take measures to minimize the damage.

Builders dislike trees because they're difficult to work around and preserve. Most builders will tell you they'd rather knock down every tree that might impede the swift completion of the task and plant new ones after the work is done. This is actually not a bad plan, especially if you can work a compromise whereby the builder makes an extra effort to spare a few mature trees in exchange for your sacrificing some of the oldsters for saplings. One of the advantages of owning a log home is that you're likely to live there a long time, so you'll be able to enjoy a tree that takes 15 to 20 years to mature. Just don't ever let that tree be a Bradford pear or any other quick-growing species with a short lifespan.

Construction workers love to store materials beneath trees. The result can often be broken branches or bark, exposing trees to disease or insect infestation. Even if you tape off trees to eliminate direct contact, heavy materials piled beneath trees well away from the trunk may cause even more harm by damaging the roots. Tree roots are sensitive. And they spread out way beyond the trunk, especially if they are trees that have been growing in a forest environment, which uncleared rural land tends to be.

Never, ever have your logs unloaded and stored beneath trees you hope to spare. The enemy isn't just materials stored beneath the trees, but also heavy equipment moving over it and compacting the soil. Bulldozers and cranes are obvious culprits, but so are pickup trucks and workbenches for power saws. The problem is that the damage is often unnoticed when it occurs, and affected trees may take a year or two to show the effects. That's too late to tell your builder, "Hey, you owe me a tree."

A few other measures you can take to lessen the impact on your trees:

▶ If the spot you selected for your building site is dense with trees that you prize, consider relocating to one whose trees you won't miss as much.

▶ Before you begin clearing the site, identify any nearby trees you wish to save. But be practical. The closer to the actual building site they are, the younger they should be. Few old trees can withstand the stress. Also, don't worry about saving trees that already are diseased or overmature or will overhang future buildings and driveways.

▶ Try to save a mix of species and in groups rather than lone strays.

▶ Enlist the help of an arborist or consult your local Cooperative Extension Service, but definitely work with your contractor and make sure all workers and subcontractors are aware of the plan.

▶ Identify construction-free zones with plastic fencing, not crime-scene tape. Mark not just the trees you want to spare, but also the extent of their underground root systems that need protection. Some people say the roots take up as much space below the ground as the crown does above. Others caution that the roots spread out as wide as the tree is tall. Still others recommend protecting the surrounding ground for

up to two times the tree's height. Whatever zone you establish, make sure everyone understands no activity or materials are allowed inside it, not even lunch breaks.

- Place a foot-thick layer of wood chips over any area near trees that will need to be walked over or have materials stored on. Take the same measure for areas where you anticipate planting new trees after you move in.

- Be vigilant at the site to make sure your wishes are known and heeded. Once you establish the rules, allow no exceptions.

- After construction, give the trees nearest the work zone extra care. Mulch, prune, fertilize and water attentively for several years. ❀

See Your Land from the Sky

Some people planning a log home have been known to drag a stepladder onto their property to stand on to check out the view so they'll know where to put the windows. It's a start. But why not take an even higher-up look to put the house in context?

A bird's-eye perspective can enhance the mental picture that you're trying to form of your home as you design it. It might even prompt some significant modifications to your plan before you break ground.

Nothing beats flying over the site. A helicopter is best, but a small single-engine plane circling slowly will also open your eyes. If you aren't a pilot, hire one. Small airports are scattered across the countryside. Chances are one is near where you intend building.

"The aerial view," William Langewiesche observes, "lets us see ourselves in context, creatures not outside nature but its most expressive agent." His book, *Inside the Sky: A Meditation on Flight*, explores the idea of learning to see from above and concludes that it is more a state of mind than a physical act.

Langewiesche proclaims the greatest explorer of the aerial view to be John Brinkerhoff Jackson, who in 1951 founded *Landscape*, a small magazine about human geography. Jackson, Langewiesche explains, practiced "in a large sense, not just the view from an airplane in flight but the habit that it breeds—a frank and distant way of seeing one's surroundings even when on the ground." Jackson himself observed: "It is from the air that the true relationship between the natural and the human landscape is first clearly revealed."

A bird's-eye perspective can enhance the mental picture that you're trying to form of your home as you design it.

Try it yourself. Start by flying over places that you're already familiar with from the ground to accustom yourself to this new way of seeing. Then head to the land you bought or are thinking of buying for your log home. As you approach it, pick out the spot you have in mind on which to build. Notice its relationship to the surrounding terrain and topography. You'll see how much a part of its setting the house will be.

Flying over land you like, even before you buy it, reveals any patterns of development. Some rural areas can be surprisingly dense, but the trees and hills might conceal the congestion on the ground. From the air, you can spot the path of progress and whether it's headed your way.

When you arrive at the site, drop down to 1,500 or 1,000 above the ground and take a really good look around. If it's a large lot, flying over it will give you a sense of its expanse. If you haven't already picked out a spot for the house,

this view might reveal one—or show you how wrong the one you've already picked is.

Notice patterns of shade and sun. Find a clearing to build your home that will minimize cutting down trees. Don't look at just the trees. Take in all the natural features: rocks, water, fields, hills and valleys. Locate any artificial features, too: roads, poles, cell-phone towers, nearby buildings, landfills.

Snap pictures. Aerial reconnaissance can significantly improve the siting of your house. A knoll or a stand of trees, especially to the north, might provide a windbreak in winter. If you've wisely decided to orient your house with the long sides facing north and south, you'll see the distant implications of this arrangement.

A closer-in look can also suggest the locations of windows, porches, garage and driveways.

As for the house itself, the aerial view will focus your attention on the roof by suggesting a style, texture and color that harmonize with the land around it. Even if only the birds appreciate this effort, your home will fit in even better.

Certainly you can design a beautiful house that meets all your expectations without considering how it looks from the sky. Adding this extra dimension, however, can only improve your design, even if the highest you ever get is standing on your tiptoes. ✿

Assemble Your Dream Team Early

13

The process of getting your log home may seem sequential: Buy your land, design your home, buy your logs and other materials, clear your land, build your home, furnish and landscape it, live happily ever after. Indeed, many people proceed on that basis and are satisfied with the results. Even though the project unfolds in this order and each stage toward your goal involves the services of a different expert, however, there is usually considerable overlap. Plus, people who don't play a part until later need to follow the same game plan as the starters. Plus, you never know what insight different people can offer each other.

You may benefit from a team approach. The usual team comprises a home designer, general contractor, builder, log producer or its sales representative, interior designer and landscape architect. You may not need the services of the last two, and your log producer may have a design staff to draw up the plans for your home, so sometimes a team can be as small as two people, plus, of course, you. It's remotely possible, if your log-home company sales representative is also a builder or you're buying a handcrafted home from a small company, that you'll be working with a one-person team. Whatever the case may be, team members invariably have their own teams. Your log producer, for example, could have a designer to draw the plans, a production coordinator to plan the cutting of the logs, a line staff to mill the logs, and a shipping department to load your logs and other materials onto a truck to deliver it, and the truck driver. But the people you'll be dealing with directly will represent whatever area they oversee. Here is the roster of your team members and their roles.

Home Designer

This is the person who will turn the ideas that you've gathered into plans for the home. By the way, your designer needn't be an architect. Many log-home companies also provide design services. Occasionally their in-house designer is an architect, but even if not, the person is likely to be familiar with the company's product's capabilities. Most log-home designs are modifications of existing plans in the company's database, and the in-house designer or draftsperson can call up the plan on a computer, order the changes and show you the results. Even if you don't intend to modify a stock plan, chances are that your ideas will closely resemble one.

Using a company's in-house designer is certainly cheaper than hiring an architect. That doesn't mean the service is free. Some companies include the design in the cost of the log package. Others charge a nominal fee, which may be credited toward the price of the home, providing, of course, that you buy from the company.

There are also independent home designers. They may even work with builders, an arrangement commonly known as design-build. Your log-home company sales representative may even offer design-build services, in which case the rep will have a pretty good understanding of log-home design. A home designer isn't the same as an architect.

But don't dismiss the idea of hiring an architect just because one costs money. Architects often save you much more than their fee by offering construction management to see that the home is built according to plan and that your project stays on time and on budget. Few architects specialize in log-home design, however, so it's essential that they understand your

> The money we spent on an architect was one of the best investments we made. And he is the one who sited the house properly for passive solar. Coming from the city, we didn't realize how important this would be in the Colorado winters.
>
> Masterson Family
> Masonville, Colorado

log producer's requirements and capabilities. What's more, even though architectural drawings are much more detailed than log-home company plans, the log producers usually have to redraw the plans to make them work with their log styles and building systems.

You can already see the benefit of having the architect or other designer working with your log producer at the outset. You don't want to pay a lot of money for a design that won't work well with logs, such as one that's modernistic, angular, predominantly glass or features lots of small, enclosed rooms. But don't think for a moment that your producer will try to dumb down your plans. Most log-home companies take pride in their logs and the finished homes, as you might have figured out from the photos they post on their web sites. For that reason, they welcome the challenge of providing logs for a showcase home.

"I had been a general contractor before, but I didn't do it this time to save money. It was more for quality control. I wanted to be able to interview and hire all the subcontractors. I checked all references. I also selected and approved all the materials. I was on the job every single day."

Morrin Family
Northwest Montana

By the way, you can design your own log home, at least in a sense. Almost every company tells the sketch-on-the-napkin story, how the customer showed up with a rough drawing that the company turned into a beautiful home. But you can be more sophisticated than that. Ordinary graph paper works well, but so do inexpensive computer

software home-design programs, at least preliminarily. Anything you come up with will have to be redrawn anyway, so don't feel tempted to buy a new super-duper computer and a $10,000 (minimum) professional log-home drafting program and enroll in architectural school, all to learn how to design just for one house. Whenever you feel inclined to head down such paths, refer to *Chapter 1: Keep Your Eye on the Prize.*

Log Producer or Sales Representative

Some homebuyers deal directly with their log-home company, but most work through company reps. These reps may be company employees or independent agents. Whatever their business arrangement, they will serve as your liaison with the company. I'll elaborate later on their services and value to you, but from a team standpoint, they can tell you what's possible with the logs.

You may think of a log home as completely different from all other types of homes, but it's only the log part that's different. Windows are windows, floors are floors, and kitchen sinks are kitchen sinks. The bulk of your log home, in fact, will be materials other than logs. How they are integrated with the logs, however, is crucial. Having someone on the team to explain what logs can, can't and shouldn't do is a real asset to those working with logs for the first time or working with your log-home company and its way of using logs. Even experienced log-home designers and builders may be unfamiliar with your company's logs. If so, they'll have plenty of questions, and the earlier on that they get the answers they need, the quicker and smoother the project will proceed.

Will your builder pay close attention to the small details?

General Contractor

This team member plays the pivotal role: turning your plans and logs into the finished home. GCs are more managers than hands-on performers, and they handle all the money matters, such as getting bids and estimating costs, and scheduling deliveries and subcontractors. The GC supervises all the work but may not be on the job site the whole time. GCs that are experienced with log construction will know what's involved in terms of materials and labor and can offer plenty of logistical suggestions as the project is being planned.

It is the general contractor's job to hire subcontractors. These workers handle projects from digging leach fields and excavating foundations to installing flooring and covering the roof. Usually they work in sequence rather than all at once, and the GC handles the juggling act of workers and the materials they need. The GC also obtains all necessary permits.

Builder

Sometimes builders act as the GC, especially on smaller jobs when they can handle the work with their own crews, but in every case they are working hands-on. They usually either erect the log shell with the log producer's technical assistance or take over after the producer's crew has stacked the logs. Builders perform all the labor from then on, except where specialized subcontractors are needed, notably plumbers and electricians. These tradespeople work alongside the builders but are the responsibility of the general contractor. Whereas GCs may be handling other jobs than yours at the same time and not always exclusively at your job site, builders generally stay with the project from start to finish.

Interior Designer

Some people regard "interior design" as just a fancy-pants name for decorators and further believe that "decorators" are just shoppers that let you tag along with them while they spend your money. These people clearly don't understand what interior designers do.

Others feel that furnishing a log home is enough of a challenge that they need professional help. And interior designers are serious professionals. In fact, some states require they be licensed. Even interior designers that don't need a license have to pass a test, plus have a specified minimum of education and experience to be entitled to add the letters ASID after their professional name. That stands for American Society of Interior Designers (*www.asid.org*), which specifies ethical and professional conduct. "At all times," the ASID directs, "members must keep the health, safety and welfare of the public in mind when designing a space." That's a lot more responsibility that just going shopping.

Even fireplace mantels can be architectural statements.

So what's the difference between an interior designer and a decorator? A decorator fashions the "look" of a space and its outward decoration—paint, fabric, furnishings, light fixtures and other materials. An interior designer is professionally trained to not only enhance the total visual environment, but also create a space that is functional, efficient and safe.

Among the many aspects interior designers address are space planning and use, including organizational and storage needs; long-term project and lifestyle planning; national, state and local building code; safety and accessibility; ergonomics; design for people with special needs; "green" design; interior detailing of background elements, such as wall and ceiling designs; custom design of furniture, drapery and accessories; selection of appliances, plumbing fixtures and flooring materials; and acoustics and sound transmission. These aspects have implications that go well beyond deciding whether this color goes with that.

Making your interior designer part of the overall design process can help plan light sources (natural and artificial), nooks and built-ins that will be up to the home designer and builder to make happen. Buying furniture is a small part of the job, but if you have in mind a certain scale or even a centerpiece, such as an elaborate chandelier or a piano, then the interior designer can coordinate with the rest of the team to accommodate such items appropriately.

Landscape Architect

Think of landscape architects as the outdoor equivalent of interior designers. Their job is knowing where to place flowers, trees, walkways and other landscape details. Rather than just plunk down plants where they might look good, they develop a thorough site plan and a schedule for its development over many years. They analyze the surroundings and take into account the weather, soil type, terrain, any water and existing vegetation. They see where sunlight falls at different times.

Just as house designers draw up plans for the home, landscape architects draw what they want the landscape to look like, using computers, sketches, models and photographs to show clients what the land will look like when the plans are finished. They also estimate how much their plan will cost and compile a list of needed materials.

The biggest challenge for landscape architects working on a log home is choosing plantings and features that will work in a low-maintenance or non-manicured setting. Even owners of log homes as their primary residence often prefer a setting that employs native grasses rather than tended lawns. And there's the inevitable and perplexing problem of protecting growth from wildlife, particularly deer.

Having your landscape architect working with other team members from the outset can resolve two issues: terrain and trees. Earth-moving equipment can alter a site to the landscaper's advantage, and the landscaper can work with the construction crew to save as many trees as are needed for the final plan. Adding new features, such as ponds, is also work best done, or at least started, as the site is being cleared.

There are two other possible team members.

Project Manager

Some log-home buyers hire a project manager to assemble and oversee the team and coordinate the effort. The advantage is that the project manager is on the job handling all the details from start to finish. Project managers can go so far as to find you a log producer to supply your package.

Lender

Some people consider lenders team members. If their role is just to approve your loan, they don't bring much to the table in terms of interaction with other players. Plus, they usually do their job before you get started on your project. They might prove helpful if they're skeptical about the project itself by advocating on your behalf for loan approval after having your log-home company representative and builder sit down with them, explain the project and show their credentials to demonstrate that you're taking this undertaking seriously.

It's conceivable that if you're asking to borrow more than the bank is willing to lend, the loan officer can work with the other team members to figure out how to trim the budget to everyone's satisfaction.

Your team must address certain issues pertaining to the home's planning and construction. The key isn't how many team members there are but having everyone on board before you begin planning and building your home. Doing so will make the process go smoother and allow everyone to benefit from each other's experience and different needs.

However you assemble your team, remember that you are the leader. Try to ensure cooperation among the players, but resolving conflict is up to you. In some cases, you may be performing one or more of the assigned roles. In other cases, you may never set foot on the site until the home is completely finished and furnished. In every case, however, the final decision is yours. ❁

Design for Yourself and Your Lifestyle   14

The way we live in a house is usually a response to the way the house is. A log home is a custom design that can be lived in any way you decide. That decision will largely dictate your design.

Designing your log home is easily the most challenging part of the buying-and-building process. The reason should be obvious. Few people are able to visualize a home, any kind of home, and translate that vision into detailed plans to guide its erection.

To some degree, a log home doesn't look all that different from any ordinary house. They both have walls and a roof, windows and doors. Inside, there are no special "log-home" rooms, just the same rooms you'd find in any home of comparable size.

Still, it is a log home. And even though logs are only the building material, log homes do exhibit certain conventions. These aren't requirements, just features that many log-home owners favor. Log homes tend to have open layouts, great rooms, walls of windows framing a view, expansive decks or porches and few hallways. In general, log homes have an air of informality.

The biggest difference about log-home design is that you're going to design your home, not drive up to a lot with a pre-designed house already built on it. This is an exciting opportunity but a formidable challenge.

It's also why you spent all that time familiarizing yourself with different log-home looks and gathering photographs and floor plans. Remember *Chapter 5: Gather Ideas?*

There was also *Chapter 8: Know When and How to Compromise?* That discussed the economics of design from the standpoint of adjustments to your home plans to make your budget work. The important message was that the simpler your design, the cheaper the home will be to build.

"Our great room fireplace uses gas log inserts. We didn't want to deal with hauling in wood. We also didn't use a raised hearth. It's flush with the floor so that we have more room. Putting all three fireplaces on the outside walls also took up less space."

Berry Family
Estes Park, Colorado

With those points in mind as you begin designing your home, you should be generally familiar with the way log homes look and feel somewhat confident about undertaking the design of your log home. When setting out to design a log home, you're considering two facets. One is layout. The other is look. The look is the general three-dimensional presentation of the home: its shape, size and proportions. The layout is how the space is allocated within this form and the relationship of the spaces. Your aim is to come up with a look that says "log home" and a layout that promotes a flow for the way you expect to live in your log home.

The best place to start planning how to apportion the space in your new home is to assess your current living situation. List all the features you like and dislike. Almost everyone wants more space, but that doesn't necessarily mean more rooms. Sometimes what's really needed is better arrangement of the same amount of space or even less.

When you bought your existing home, you probably didn't have the opportunity to specify exactly where you wanted every room, every closet and every window. In your log home, you will enjoy this privilege.

By analyzing your current situation, you will discover immediately some traps to avoid. Are you tired of climbing stairs every night from the living room to your bedroom? In your new log home, you can place the master bedroom right beside the living room, on the same level. Instead of having to lug laundry from the bedrooms to the washer-dryer at the far end of the kitchen, now you can plan a laundry room closer to the bedrooms—or even in the basement with a dumbwaiter system to lower dirty clothes and raise clean clothes within a few steps of the dressers and closets where they will be put away.

You can personalize your design as much as you like. If you want half the total square footage devoted to a kitchen or a master suite, by all means indulge yourself. Keep in mind, however, that going too far overboard may limit your ability to sell if you decide or are forced to move. Again, this is where looking at pictures can help.

Of course, certain common-sense notions prevail. It isn't such a good idea to build the garage next to the master bedroom on the other side of the house from the kitchen. This is not to say that you can't arrange your rooms this way, if it's really what you want. After all, this will be your house.

The biggest mistake people make when they are planning a layout for a log home is including way too many hallways. If you're sure you want them, go ahead. Most people, however, find that a better arrangement, even in compartmentalized layouts, is having rooms flow directly into each other. You can refine the layout as you go along, but identifying situations to avoid at the outset will increase your satisfaction—and prevent costly revisions, either on paper or once construction is under way.

It's instructive but certainly not mandatory to know something about the evolution of log-home design. The pioneers who built frontier log cabins didn't worry about whether the master bedroom had its own wing or was grouped with the other bedrooms because their aim was basic shelter. The entire floor plan was one rectangular, open space. Windows were impractical, costly and superfluous. The first interior walls were probably blankets hung from a rope stretched from one wall to its opposite. Food was prepared outside the house or in the same fireplace as heated the home. Toilets were holes in the ground outside.

As people settled, houses revealed more planning. One of the most engrossing and amusing stories involving log-home design is a novel by Donald Harington, titled *The Architecture of the Arkansas Ozarks*. It tells the tale of the town of Stay More, beginning with its settlement by brothers Jacob and Noah Ingledew. The saga follows the principals and their heirs for six generations, illustrating the town's early progress by its log architecture, from crude cabin to dogtrot to hewn home.

Another illustrative record is *The Hewn Log House* by Charles McRaven. The author, an experienced and articulate log-home renovator, working mostly with 19th-century structures, is responsible for showing that the first log homes were actually well-along affairs, not the crude pioneer cabins commonly assumed. You can still witness evidence for yourself in the hills and valleys of Appalachia. A day's drive on U.S. Route 11, which parallels Interstate 81 along Virginia's historic and scenic Shenandoah Valley, takes you through town after town populated by hefty hewn-log homes. These were usually two-story buildings, which have survived since before the American Revolution. Many more exist than are seen because it became the custom to sheath these homes in siding to conceal that they were built of logs, which became a mark of frontier crudeness that was embarrassing in a society striving to better itself.

As traditional as log cabins and hewn houses were, they aren't what people aspire to nowadays. Some people have successfully updated them, either by combining several log structures or incorporating the log building into a larger, conventional building. No doubt the hewn logs, already 200-plus years old, would outlast any contemporary species, but they are likelier to endure in some different form, such as plank flooring.

Because the advent of sawmilling and balloon framing pretty much spelled the end of log building in settled communities, few new log homes

> "I always wanted wood floors, but after finally having them in our previous log home, I realized I like carpeting and tile for a change of pace from the log walls and because they're so much easier to keep clean than wood floors."
>
> Reedy Family
> Warren, Ohio

were built until the 1970s. Log-home design didn't really begin until then. Sure, grand lodges and great camps had been built in mountain settings, but these were playhouses for the rich. Smaller camps and cabins popped up in wood and beside lakes in the early 20th century, but these rarely strayed from rudimentary designs.

As the building material achieved popularity in the late 1970s and early 1980s, log homes advanced from cabins to primary residences. As such, they needed to fulfill the expectations of their owners, who definitely were not backwoods folk. Contemporary log-home design began with embellishments to the basic rectangle.

At first, pickings were slim. As engineering stretched the limits of how logs could be configured and how to integrate solid-wood walls

with expanses of glass, however, log homes achieved the level of true custom design. Many of the standard plans that log-home companies offer today originated as custom designs that caught on with buyers.

There are design conventions, some regional, others reaching across boundaries. Design also takes its cue from a variety of other influences. As the possibilities have grown, rules have ceased to exist. Architects have taken up the challenge of designing log homes that combine wood and the imagination. Some of their creations are true masterpieces. Others are monuments to their own egos or the extravagance of their clients.

For all the possibilities, truly successful log homes stress livability. And not just any livability. The best home is one that lives the way you do. Or the way you intend to live. Just be sure you know how that is.

If you'll be designing your log home for your retirement years, for example, how different do you anticipate those times being from the way you live now? When clients meet with an architect to discuss their expectations for their new log home, atop most every wish list is a larger kitchen. In some cases, they want a huge kitchen with a full array of culinary accessories. Now that they're leaving the rat race, they expect to be entertaining friends and family often, even though they'll be building the home hundreds of miles from where their friends and family live, and, on top of everything else, they've always hated cooking. What they really enjoy is television, movies and music. The solution is a smaller, galley kitchen and a large media room. The few times a year they do have company, they can cook outdoors or take their guests to a local restaurant.

"If you'll be living more than half an hour from town, put in a bigger kitchen and pantry than you think you need. You'll be cooking at home more."

Phillips Family
Bellvue, Colorado

The lesson is that people rarely change their lives as radically as they intend. They usually merely amplify aspects of their existing lifestyles. Active people will crave more activity. Couch potatoes just want bigger couches.

One aspect of moving into a log home that will change your point of view is the surroundings. The land around a log home usually merits looking at, so you'll probably want to incorporate design features that allow you to enjoy near and distant views: larger window groupings, decks and porches.

Being able to determine the look of your home ranks alongside choosing its location for most log-home buyers. You can experience for yourself the adventure of designing your log home. Your plan can be as practical or as fanciful as you wish. If money is

no object, indulge your whims. If you must watch costs, apply ingenuity. Even the most extravagant log-home owner delights in proudly pointing out some self-devised or realized shortcut that saved a dollar or two.

Successful design rarely is attained without revision. Compromise is unavoidable. People who hire a professional designer often accede to that person's will because they feel unqualified and thus unworthy to criticize what purports to be professional interpretation of their vision. But if what some architect shows you isn't what you have in mind, you won't be happy living in it.

Professionals are trained to solve problems creatively, but their solution might not be the best for you. Don't be intimidated by credentials. No matter how impressive a designer's portfolio may be or how close your working relationship is with that person, regard the expert as your hired hand. If what emerges isn't totally to your liking, say so. If something you are shown inspires modification, make your views known. ❁

Look Around for Inspiration

Houses don't just happen. They have to be envisioned before they can be built. Design can be purposeful or inspired. Purposeful design is practical. It may seek to improve livability or control construction costs. Inspired design is fanciful. Its aim is distinction.

Houses are almost never imagined in a vacuum. Other houses or a particular setting usually influence their look.

Don't misunderstand what design is. Good looks aren't necessarily good flow. The size and relationship of rooms create the floor plan. This is a two-dimensional depiction of the house. It indicates, let's say, how big the living room will be, whether it will be in the front of the house or the back, and if it will open to the kitchen or be separated by a wall.

People often assume that once they agree on a layout, they have designed their home. Houses consist of more than square footage, however. Imagining a home in three dimensions is a challenge.

We usually muddle through life oblivious to the visual clutter around us. Unless you're an architect or a professional designer, the way different houses look seems irrelevant. Once you begin considering a custom log home, however, design should become part of your everyday reality.

Look around. Carry a camera and look for houses to photograph. Notice shapes, sizes, rooflines and all exterior trappings. Shoot any features that appeal to you.

If you live somewhere totally removed from where you anticipate building, take advantage of other people's photography. Peruse magazines that show log homes in the kind of setting you desire. Notice how homes and surroundings harmonize.

Imagining a home in three dimensions is a challenge.

Setting may also evoke a design that makes the new house look well established on the site. This tendency toward timelessness is particularly popular with owners of traditional-looking log homes.

Besides conjuring up an image of a house, the setting may even suggest a layout. If the home will enjoy a compelling view, for instance, then the design may not only include plenty of windows facing this view, but also feature a layout that enables most of the rooms to share the view. The resulting profile would be a narrow and either a long or tall house.

Climate also influences design. Hot sun prompts porches. Heavy snow dictates a steep roof. Constant wind calls for streamlining.

Expanding your design horizons will guide you toward a look that suits your tastes and location. Having a vision will bring you that much closer to turning your plan into an actual home. ❁

Design for Protection   15

Wood in use must be protected from the elements. This instruction is particularly directed at log homes, whose exterior wood surfaces are constantly exposed. Twenty years ago, most log-home buyers lacked this crucial knowledge. In fact, unscrupulous log-home salespeople often touted log homes as "maintenance free."

Fortunately, reputable log-home companies and the makers of sealants, coatings and wood preservatives acted before much damage resulted to the structures and to the reputation of log homes in general. Understanding how wood fares over time and what specific protection logs require resulted in products that are very effective in protecting your investment. (See the appendix: *Preserve Your Home's Good Looks.*)

You can improve the service life of these products and thus reduce maintenance costs by purposeful design to protect your logs' exterior surfaces from the weather, specifically the effects of precipitation (rain and melting snow) and sunlight (harmful ultraviolet radiation). These are tried-and-true tactics. Even ancient log construction, known to have occurred before 700 B.C. in Eastern Europe, used certain techniques to protect log structures from insects and decay: special corner notches that shed water, organic coatings that blocked water penetration and retarded fungal growth, and such practical innovations as large roof overhangs and stone foundations.

Designing your home for protection begins with properly positioning the home on the site so rainwater and melting snow will drain away from the surface on all sides. If this is not possible or desirable, alter natural drainage by using swales and berms, retaining walls, ditches or sub-surface drain tiles before you begin construction. Once the house is built, install gutters to move water away from the house. Be sure these gutters and downspouts are made of non-combustible materials.

Keep your logs well off the ground. Earth-to-wood contact invites decay fungi and termites. Plan to build the foundation wall at least three feet above grade to eliminate any possibility of logs' coming into contact with the ground and to prevent rainwater or mud from splashing on the logs.

Don't overlook landscaping. Avoid planting shrubs that will come in contact with the wall logs and delay drying, or rub against the logs in the wind. Elsewhere, use common sense to prevent the introduction of insects through mulch and plantings. If you build on a site with thick trees, consider thinning them to let some sunlight through to promote drying and thwart mildew.

Protect exterior log surfaces with wide roof overhangs, at least 18 to 24 inches for a one-story home and 24 to 36 inches for a two-story home. Wider is better. Moisture from rain, melting snow and even condensation can run down the face of the log wall and move in and through any cracks that might occur in the log. Overhangs are particularly crucial at the corners to protect exposed log ends and prevent water from pooling on the top of the corner logs, especially in intersecting corner styles using logs with relatively flat tops. Consider corner styles that promote quick drainage.

Incidentally, because log homes built in woodland settings may be at risk from wildfires, build or reinforce overhangs with fire-resistant materials because they can trap flames, heat and smoke. Roofing materials that resist fire best are brick, masonry, slate, clay or concrete tile, exposed concrete

"I'd recommend building decks and railings out of composite material or rot-resistant wood. Don't use pine unless you feel like replacing it after five or six years."

Phillips Family
Bellvue, Colorado

deck, ferrous or copper shingle and panel roof coverings, according to the National Roofing Contractors Association. Metal sheet or shingle roof systems are next best, followed by asphalt-composition shingles, treated wood shingles and cold-applied built-up roofing (layers of roll roofing bonded together with adhesive). The roofing material you choose will likely affect your homeowner's insurance rates, thus lowering the actual cost of higher-quality roofing.

For the same reason, avoid designing a home with any ledges that can retain water. Be especially careful with the tops of any door and window trim or any other projections that ultimately link to the logs, whether directly or downhill. Some log styles have drip edges to ensure that water running down one log will not find its way between it and the log beneath it.

Porches also are effective ways to protect logs from both water and sunlight.

Fortunately, these protective measures can also enhance your home's

appearance. By elevating your logs off the ground, for example, you expose enough of the foundation wall that can be covered with natural or manufactured stone to provide a pleasing transition from the ground to the logs.

You can make the effect even more dramatic by tying in this stone with that used for a chimney or for pilasters supporting posts, such as those for the entry or a rear deck.

Extending the roof can enhance your home's profile. And gutters can provide a colorful accent that ties in with door and window trim or the roof. There are even pressure-treated wooden gutters that can add a distinctively rustic look.

And a porch that protects the southwest-facing wall or walls, which receive the most exposure from the sun, adds a harmonious architectural feature that many people find an essential part of the log-home look. As a bonus, a well-designed porch providing maximum UV protection also offers a pleasant place to sit in the evening and take in magnificent sunsets. ✿

Large eaves are ideal in the heavy-snow country of the Pacific Northwest.

Design for the Future 16

Log homes are the ultimate move-up home. People tend to live in them for many years, sometimes long enough to pass down to grown children and their families. Design your home to accommodate how you expect to live when you first move in and anticipate how you might live as the years pass. Planning your log home means looking beyond its construction. Lives change. So should your log home.

Consider how your home might grow. Additions aren't especially difficult for log homes, but they have to be planned.

The folly of not planning is evident in any single-family housing development older than 20 years. People who need more room gain it with a jumble of juts that often offend sensibilities and violate building codes. Don't succumb to expediency. You won't have to if you approach the initial design of your log home with some foresight.

Plan additions so they'll go with your design. If they're never needed or afforded, no problem. The home will look coherent without them, not like some unfinished municipal works project awaiting public funding. If they are needed, though, they'll fit in with the original home, and not look like some tacky tack-on.

Finishing off a basement is the easiest, cheapest way to increase livable space. Adding a second story to a ranch-style log home isn't too difficult, unless you intend to make it full-log construction. But there's the problem of the extra load on the existing house, particularly the logs, which have settled snugly into their new position. You don't want to upset them.

Whereas when building a log home, you're better off building up or down, when it comes to additions, building out is usually the most sensible strategy. There are two factors to consider: tying the new part in with the old and matching the logs.

Usually your log addition will settle, but your existing logs long ago stabilized. You don't want the new wing dragging the old home down. A common technique is to create a stud-framed link between the different parts. This can be a small spacer to accommodate the transition or a full-size room connecting the two parts. You might be inspired to fashion some kind of breezeway that creates a dogtrot-style home.

Matching the logs is a snap if your original log producer is still in business. Just order more of the same. But unless you used something really odd, any producer ought to be able to match the profile and wood species.

To prevent the addition from sticking out, clean the exterior of the logs of the original home before the addition is built. Really clean them, though, using a corn blaster or some other method that won't rip off the log surface. Then, when the addition is finished, coat the entire structure at the same time with the same product.

One way around additions is outbuildings. If you reach the stage where you find your home is too small for your guests, build a guesthouse. A smaller version of your main house will work. Depending on the look of the main house, a quaint, old-timey cabin might make an especially welcoming annex. Even a detached garage with a second-story apartment will work—and you can cover it with log siding that resembles your full logs.

Planning goes beyond the outside. If you intend having stud-framed interior walls, lay them out so they can be removed to enlarge rooms or added to compartmentalize space as your needs change. A children's wing, for example, might have three or four bedrooms arranged so that

"With a teenager still living with us, a media room was a must-have on our list. This fit perfectly in the bonus space above the garage. We added a full bath in case we ever decided to sell and the new owners wanted another guest suite."

Cronacher Family
Jackson Hole, Wyoming

as each child grows up and leaves home, walls can be removed to enlarge the rooms of the children that remain. Similarly, for a growing family, a big, open wing can be subdivided to create separate bedrooms for each new child. The key when planning interior space is to allow for some flexibility.

Flexibility also applies to how you will live in your home as the years pass. Plan for natural and unexpected changes to your physical condition to ensure maximum enjoyment and use of your home throughout the time you spend in it. Here are some features to incorporate into your plans.

> **All main living space on one level.** That way, if climbing stairs becomes difficult, you won't have to go up and down every day, only occasionally to clean guest rooms.

> **Wide doorways and hallways.** These features work exceptionally well in log homes because of the popularity of open layouts. Log homes often have wide, carved archways between rooms that not only enhance mobility, but also add distinction to the interior look of the home.

"I wish we would've built our garage twice as big or planned for a storage shed. We didn't know we'd need all the miscellaneous equipment that is essential to living in the mountains."

Masterson Family
Masonville, Colorado

- **Easy-to-reach cabinets, appliances and counters.** Adjustable shelving and movable fixtures increase access.
- **Layouts that allow adequate space for mobility**, especially in kitchens and bathrooms.
- **Ample lighting** (natural and artificial), with less glare and easy-to-operate switches.
- **High-seat toilets and sit-down showers**.
- **No-step access or thresholds from room to room**.

Think in terms of moving stuff from one level to another and try to lighten your load. If your laundry room is on one level but all your bedrooms on another, consider a laundry chute so you don't have to carry dirty linens.

This concept also applies to carrying yourself. A few homeowners have built closets on separate levels but in the same location so that if the time comes when climbing stairs proves too difficult, they can install an elevator where the closets are.

Universal design, also called barrier-free or accessible design, involves

more than just building a switchback ramp from ground level to your front door. It accommodates not only diversity in general human function, but also the changes that occur as the result of aging, illness or injury. It is a way of incorporating features that allow you to continue using your home longer and allow guests with limited mobility to enjoy visits. The principles, methods and goals of universal design are now well enough known that most architects are familiar with them and can apply them to your log home as they would to any home.

You don't want to live like you're in your eighties when you're only in your fifties, but universal design isn't just for seniors. It provides convenience of all ages by ensuring comfort, easier maintenance and maximum mobility. Above all, these design features will make your log home easy to enter, use, enjoy and entertain in for the rest of your life. ❁

Gain bonus space by enclosing peaks of cathedral ceilings while keeping log rafters and ridge beam for a log touch.

Power Outages?

Living out of town, you will experience more power outages, and they will take longer to repair. To be prepared, you should consider installing a backup generator. Larger generators are stationary and usually mounted on a concrete pad next to the house. Smaller generators are portable and can be stored in a shed or garage. Fuel choices are propane, gas or diesel. Electricians can help you determine which critical loads in your home to power and will wire a subpanel accordingly. They can also recommend what size of generator to buy (rated by watts). ❁

17 Think Inside the Box

Just because you're custom designing your log home doesn't mean you have to reinvent the box. There are only so many ways you can configure log walls, and most of those configurations have already been tried and tested.

Most log-home companies have a stock of plans that their customers choose from. Many of these plans may have originated as custom designs for a client, and the company recognized the plan might also appeal to future customers, so they incorporated it into their plans library. That doesn't mean subsequent versions turn out identically.

It's easy to look at a stock plan and regard it as already perfect. That's why it ended up being published in a plans book. The trick is to recognize a plan that has the potential to become perfect for you, then figure out exactly which changes to make.

Almost all stock plans are modified to some degree to suit customers' preferences. Working within the same footprint, buyers may move walls, switch rooms and otherwise change dimensions and configurations. Log-home company designers use computerized drafting equipment to quickly adjust any standard plan to your liking—and even combine the most appealing features of several plans.

The most common changes to stock plans are adding or deleting square footage; adding or deleting porches and decks; changing window and door locations, shapes and sizes; adding, deleting or rearranging interior walls; and adding garages, workshops, mud rooms and breezeways. Many times, what may be perceived as a small and simple change by the homebuyer can end up being a very complex and costly change due to the overall effect the change may have due to structural reasons. For example, you may want to eliminate a post that is supporting the roof. Accomplishing this might require the roof system to be totally redesigned, using different and more costly materials.

But just because you customize a plan to meet your requirements doesn't necessarily mean it will be more expensive. Cost depends on how carried away you get. By the time you add two feet here and raise the log wall one course there, add a dormer or two and upgrade to a new log style, the cost savings of building a stock plan is gone. In this regard, a totally custom-designed home can actually be cheaper and more functional if all factors, criteria and considerations are analyzed and incorporated from scratch.

Stock plans that are very fanciful and difficult to build can be made even more difficult and expensive by trying to force them onto unobliging sites.

The building site affects many factors. Above all, the layout and shape of the house must conform to the site and its terrain. Log homes are generally built on larger parcels of land, and very seldom is that land flat.

When matching a building site to a particular stock plan, consider three factors:

1. **The septic tank, leach field and the well.** Their locations will determine the specific spot on your lot for the home, thereby influencing its size and shape.

2. **Views.** The best vantage points will determine positioning of the home and placement of rooms and windows.

3. **Roads and driveways.** The approach route to the house will affect its configuration, as well as the location of the front door.

Each of these site factors may require or inspire you to modify the stock plan you like. The problem is that some changes can have serious repercussions on the construction of the house. With all the other considerations given to size and function of rooms, orientation to the site and terrain, the views and southern exposure, it's very difficult to find a stock plan that meets those criteria, to say nothing about family size, age, and entertaining family and friends, formally or informally. Add one more all-important consideration: personal expression.

The key to choosing an appropriate stock plan is affordability. Telling a log-home company not just what you need and want, but also how much you can pay, will help the company direct you toward plans in your price range. One way to ensure greater satisfaction if you're on a limited budget is to find out how you can get more home for your dollar. For example, a story-and-a-half or two-story home costs less per square foot than a ranch style. Choosing a home up to 28 feet wide is more cost effective because it uses standard material sizes.

Another point is your lifestyle. Couples with children may want a bedroom for each child, as well as the convenience of a separate master bath,

"Our log-home company suggested that for just a little Sheetrock and carpet, we could turn the space above our bedroom from attic storage into a great loft area. Today, it is one of our most favorite rooms. Every time I look at the loft, I say, 'I can't believe we almost didn't have this.' We use it all the time."

Gaura Family
New Salem, North Carolina

meaning perhaps a two-story home. An older couple, by contrast, might find a ranch-style home more to their liking. Looking at a variety of stock plans gives buyers with different circumstances the opportunity to determine the style and layout of a home that would best suit their needs.

When touring various sales models, it is also very helpful for you to see a floor plan of the model home you are visiting. It helps you visualize firsthand the realization of the floor plan placed before you so that when you see the plan for your house, you will have less trouble envisioning what it will look like once it is finished.

Along these lines, understand that certain modifications made to suit buyers' needs usually result in additional design and drafting costs. Your

set of plans must contain some basic elements, whether you're modifying a stock plan slightly or substantially, in order for you to secure financing, obtain the required building permits and provide contractors with a tool for estimating.

Elements of the plan include four elevations, the foundation plan, main-floor framing plan, main floor plan, second-floor framing plan, second-floor plan, roofing plan and pertinent structural sections. Additionally, each drawing includes details that illustrate and define key elements for that particular section of the house. All of these basic elements should be included, regardless of the square footage of the home.

The most challenging aspect of modifying stock plans is the time factor. Many buyers believe that because they're working from a stock set of plans, changes to these plans won't take very long. With today's computer-assisted drafting technology, modifying stock plans is relatively easy. Even so, depending on the amount of modifications required, this process could take anywhere from several hours to several days.

Some buyers purchase a kit manufacturer's floor plans, then have it produced by another company. Sometimes the producer will have to modify the plans to accommodate its own log system and may charge the buyer for this conversion. There are also copyright issues affecting the copying, distribution and resale of stock plans. Some companies register their plans, giving them exclusive rights and ownership to them. In most cases, when you purchase a set of plans, you will have the right to use those plans to build one home, regardless of who the producer or supplier is.

Although stock plans are a good starting point for your eventual design, these plans change over the years. Many that worked well in the 1970s and 1980s are outdated today. People need space for home computers, Jacuzzi tubs, walk-in showers, big-screen televisions, handicap access and guests who require their own bath. A 1,600-square-foot log home that seemed roomy enough in 1978 might need to be 1,900 square feet today to fit in all those amenities and still convey the right sense of comfort.

This raises a key point. Log homes do not have to be large or complicated to be appealing. For a smaller log home under 2,000 square feet, start with a standard design or look that suits your taste, then modify the floor plan to fit your site and your way of living.

Actually, smaller log homes are more traditional than larger ones. Making the most of storage space, display shelves, built-in cabinets, cathedral ceilings and lighting helps smaller homes appear larger by making the most of the volume.

It also helps to locate furniture and traffic patterns in a home early on in the design process because your layout options may be limited. Simplified rooflines, offsets and textures are a key to successful small-home design. The use of covered porches, decks and outdoor features helps increase the usable space of a small home.

As for larger homes, they can be boring if all the construction is the same. That's why buyers like to mix materials and construction systems in larger designs, using timber-frame construction and drywall in the interior, for example, and stone on the exterior to break up the wood while retaining the architectural theme. Large homes are not large boxes. They tend to be an aggregation of smaller boxes. Once the box has been defined, it becomes easier to mix components. Custom-designed large homes are the norm rather than the exception.

Large or small, good stock plans strive to have certain characteristics. When you are considering

Building a garage beneath the house reduces the footprint and saves on exterior building material, such as log siding.

a stock plan or a modified version of one, your plan generally has to meet four major criteria. It should be both functional and suitable to the your lifestyle, architecturally pleasing, adaptable to the chosen building site, and one that can be completely built within your budget. Because these criteria are different for each buyer, producers' stock plans vary drastically in regards to characteristics and components, the theory being that a company tries to offer something for everyone.

Buyers contemplating changes to stock plans should consider the four major criteria identified above and ask two questions:

▶ What effect will the proposed changes have on the four criteria?

▶ Do the changes have a positive effect in regards to achieving the four criteria?

If you can answer yes to this last question, then you are one step closer to having your dream log home. Always keep in mind that the only limitations are your imagination and your budget.

> "Design features we'd do next time include an upstairs balcony, a year-round sunroom, and, of course, more storage space. A covered porch would sure save on snow shoveling too."
>
> Ewing Family
> Masonville, Colorado

Above all, do your homework. The more information you give the draftsperson, the easier it will be for her or him to do the job—and for the log-home company to produce the home you want. Some of the biggest problems that occur with a buyer's design ideas are structural, such as getting all the bearing points to line up and making sure that you don't draw something that cannot be built. This is vital.

Before you begin to study actual floor plans leading to your home, try creating a plan yourself or at least make a list of what you want. Then look at log-home magazines, books and catalogs. By then you'll be ready to work with a log-home designer to make slight or major changes to a stock plan or embark on a brand-new custom design.

Whichever design route you take to your final home plan, careful planning—plus understanding what you truly need and want—can make the construction process move much more efficiently. The result will be a home that is created just for you. ✤

Choose a Company that Offers the Look You Love

18

There are dozens of log-home producers. They differ in many ways. Some are full-service manufacturing plants with computerized design departments, precision milling equipment and nationwide dealer networks. Others are a guy with a chain saw.

Usually these distinctions involve the companies' building systems, their materials packages (commonly referred to as kits), their wood species, their log profiles, corner styles, fastening and sealing systems, and a host of other technical distinctions that define their log homes as being different from each other's.

Remember the chapter on wood, how time-consuming a distraction trying to identify the best species for your logs can be? Well, you could easily drive yourself just as crazy trying to scrutinize all aspects of the way these many log companies do business and weigh the differences. So, avoid the problem. Don't be distracted by technical matters, unless you're the kind of person who, prior to buying an ordinary house, removes all the drywall to see what kind of nails are used in the studwork and how far apart the 2-by-4s are.

More important than uncovering how a company engineers its log homes is finding one whose homes look the way you'd like your log home

to and with whom you feel good about doing business. That doesn't mean you should be oblivious to the technical aspects of log-home construction, only that the nitpicky details rarely matter and needn't preoccupy you.

While gathering ideas, you found photos of homes and identified features that appealed to you. As you consider companies to produce your log home, look for ones that offer those features. Make sure these companies provide the design service you desire, as well as standard plans that will incorporate the look and layout that you determine are going to work best with your setting and your idea of what your log home should look like.

Besides finding a company that offers the look you love, dig below the surface and see what you can learn about the character of the company. Is the company one you feel good about dealing with? Does it represent its product proudly without knocking its competitors? Do you feel pressured to sign a deal before you feel ready? You want a company that can deliver the home you want, not be made to feel like you're negotiating with a used-car dealer.

After talking to the salespeople, meet the folks working behind the scenes. Arrange a tour of mills and yards. Establish a relationship that makes you feel positive about buying a home from this company. Most log-home companies have

Handcrafted logs cut and fit, then taken apart and re-stacked at the home site.

a single owner, someone who may have started out when today's log homes started becoming popular and has stuck with the business through all these years. I've spoken with many company owners who, years after selling a home, can recall details of it and its buyers. It says a lot about a company that values its customers enough to get to know them and go out of its way to ensure their satisfaction. Well-designed, well-made homes from a company with a good reputation matter more than whether its logs have one tongue and groove or two. ❀

"We didn't know of any log-home companies in the area to contact for ideas, so we just traveled around the area and identified other houses made of log. Then we would approach the owners and ask who the builder was, who the architect was and what the logs were."

O'Shea Family
Park City, Utah

19 Understand How Your Log Producer Provides for Log Settling

Oe technical matter that you will want some reassurance about, because it is the single-biggest worry of potential log-home buyers, is how your log home will settle after it's built. Settlement is so misunderstood and dreaded that some people dreaming of buying a log home decide, the moment they hear that log homes settle, that they'd rather have some other kind. Any other. In order not to lose customers, almost any company you ask will insist that every other company's homes settle, but not theirs.

Indisputable science disputes such claims, however. All buildings settle. That's gravity.

Logs shrink. That's nature.

Shrinkage isn't a problem but merely the response of wood in use, through evaporation and compression. However much or little logs shrink, companies' building systems are designed to accommodate this natural process. This accommodation is the basis of companies' claims that their logs don't settle. They might have better luck keeping customers if they told them, "Our homes settle, but we know how to deal with it."

As logs shrink, they move. Efforts to stabilize logs begin with drying methods. A soon as a tree is cut down, the moisture in the wood cells begins evaporating, and the logs—"tree cadavers," Jim Renfroe calls them in *The*

Log Home Owner's Manual: A Guide to Protecting and Restoring Exterior Wood—dry. This drying, called seasoning, continues until the remaining moisture equals the air's ambient humidity. Until then, the logs shrink.

A technical note from the Log Homes Council (LHC) defines shrinkage as "a dimensional change in wood caused by a decrease in moisture content (water) below the fiber saturation point (about 30 percent). As water leaves the cells, these cells collapse to a lesser dimension. Unless the log is dried to less than 19 percent moisture content, seasoning can continue for up to three heating seasons."

So what are the different drying methods log producers use? Some use kilns—heat sweats out moisture and fans speed evaporation—to dry their logs, thus "pre-shrinking" them, reducing their weight, making them easier to mill, crystallizing the pitch in resinous species and killing any insects or organisms that may have invaded the live tree. Some companies further warrant specific moisture content by managing kiln time and cycles accordingly.

One Tennessee manufacturer went so far as to buy a 17-foot-tall vacuum kiln capable of sucking water from 45 tons of logs at a time—that's three homes' worth—in seven to ten days. A few companies have experimented with microwaves, which dry wood from the inside out.

Logs drying in a kiln.

Another common method, air drying, involves storing timbers over time and allowing airflow to evaporate the moisture from the wood before it is used. The moisture content of air-dried wood ranges from 12 to 30 percent, depending on drying time, method and prevailing climate of the company's yard.

Others, particularly out West, use standing-dead timbers. These are logs from trees that died on the stump because of disease, beetle infestation or fire. Whatever killed them long ago left the standing

trees, leaving them thoroughly dried and ready to be selectively harvested and turned into logs. Their moisture content is at or below 20 percent when they arrive for milling, hewing or peeling.

Some companies use green or unseasoned wood, although it is usually partially air dried before it is actually used. Its moisture content is typically 30 percent or more. These companies design their homes to allow for moisture loss and shrinkage after they are built.

Other companies shape laminated beams with minimal moisture content into wall logs to reduce the log's tendency to shrink, twist, warp and check. (Checking is the longitudinal cracking of wood caused by uneven drying.)

No matter how dry the logs are, once they're stacked to form walls, the homes settle. Settling, the LHC declares, "is a natural phenomenon affected by time and the environment where the walls are built." As wall logs lose moisture, their stacked weight compacts the drying wood fibers. Even though logs are substantially heavier than lumber-and-Tyvek-wrapped regular homes, the total compression in a log home as the logs stabilize in place rarely exceeds a quarter-inch for every foot of wall height.

That fact bears noting, because it means that a 12-foot log wall isn't going to shrink more than three inches. And that shrinkage will occur only for the first three years. If your logs aren't subjected to vast temperature extremes—such as exposing them to the dry heat of furnaces and fireplaces—this shrinkage could be less.

> "Log wall settling was my biggest issue. Wherever a log wall ties into a vertical column there should be some means to lower that column as the wall settles."
>
> Benshoof Family
> Masonville, Colorado

Trust the System

Log walls aren't just the building material. They are engineered to work in conjunction with fastening and sealing systems to create a weathertight component able to adjust to log shrinkage and movement and to function as a unit. These systems allow log walls to withstand hurricanes, earthquakes, even floods far greater than most stick-built homes.

The building system addresses the fit of the logs, both horizontally and at the corners. The system also determines how the walls interact with the roof, windows and doors. The goal is to ensure the home's structural integrity.

Design services are part of the company's system and prescribe which components are to be used and how they relate. The design also takes into account how the company's logs will perform once assembled and how the fastening and sealing components will work.

Details of the building system are found in your log-home company's detailed construction manual. Even if you don't understand the manual's technical aspects, your builder should, even one who has not built log homes before. As I've stated repeatedly, different companies have different systems; everyone involved in your home's construction ought to be familiar with the specifics of your company's building system.

The system must never be compromised or deviated from. There are many different wood species, log profiles, corner styles, fasteners and sealing materials. These differences result in many possible combinations. Only one, however, will work the way the company wants it to. Substituting components or modifying the assembly risks failure. ✿

Three ways of sealing logs (from left): foam gaskets, caulk and chinking.
ILLUSTRATIONS BY THEODORA TILTON

If you like wood so much that you want it all around you, don't fret settling. Science can't overcome doubt, let alone outright dread, but it does prescribe how to manage the performance of a log wall by controlling differential settlement—the change in the height of a log wall caused by shrinkage and compression. "The settlement formula," the LHC tech note says, "varies with wood species, size and profile of log, time of year trees are cut, drying techniques (air and kiln drying), home heating and humidification, roof and floor loads, and even the occurrence of dry winds across open areas."

"As a general rule, it takes the logs up to two years to completely settle. The best situation is to wait for that period of time before the chinking is applied."

Joe Bielas, Contractor
Vancouver, Washington

Log-home companies tailor the formula to their respective building systems. They take into account log-wall connections, openings (windows and doors), and structural support posts, stairs and interior partitions. Settling also affects ceilings, fireplaces and chimneys, kitchen cabinets, electrical, plumbing and ductwork. Common ways to accommodate settlement include leaving spaces above doors and windows; these spaces are covered with trim boards that remain as the logs settle into the spaces. Another is slip joints, which let pipes and other non-attached items stay in place as the logs around them move. A more dramatic method is using screw jacks under vertical logs, which are adjusted to take up slack in the log walls as the logs settle. Remember that any settlement due to log shrinkage occurs only in the first few years.

Settling space above the window and door.

Builders and subcontractors who don't comprehend how other components interact with log walls and fail to allow for settling risk botching the home. Nobody, though, can keep stacked logs totally stable.

Whether you hurry drying or let it happen naturally, settling is inevitable. Accept it. It's what logs do. Think of them as snuggling into their new positions to gird up for the next century or two. That's at least how long log homes can stand up. And all because of wood.

Besides its remarkable strength, wood reveals a log home's personality. "One of the remarkable things about wood is its self-expression," Eric Sloane proclaims in *A Reverence for Wood*. "It is always telling something about itself. That is why man has an affinity with wood not only as a mere material, but also as a kindred spirit to live with and to know."

Who won't settle for that? ✾

"With so much stonework in the house and outside it to add character, dealing with settling was an issue. There are a lot of chimneys, for example, so we had to deal with calculations of how much to allow, because unlike the logs, stone doesn't move."

Hayes Family
Pennsylvania

Fasten-ating Rhythm

The foremost duty of any structure is to not fall down. Log homes stand up relentlessly.

You'd know that if you've been in a log home during an earthquake, a hurricane or a tornado. Whenever nature goes on one of its rampages, you never hear about log homes tumbling down. They defy disaster.

What makes log homes so reassuringly upstanding? After all, they're just chopped-down trees stacked singly on top of each other 10 feet tall or taller. And yet, they don't topple. Standing up is just what log walls do. Or must be made to do.

Since bad things usually happen when things fall apart, anything made of more than one part needs something to fasten the parts together.

Jumbo jets, for instance, depend on millions of rivets to keep all their parts flying on the same course. Log homes don't need so many fasteners, but they're all just as crucial.

You may wonder why log homes bother with fasteners since most people's reference point for log construction is the Lincoln Logs toy set. The toy walls are made by placing one log on top of another, relying on flat notches at both ends to steady them. Doesn't a real-life log home work the same?

It could, only inhabitable log homes aren't toys. They demand grown-up engineering.

Many old-timey log buildings were corner-supported, connected like Lincoln Logs toys. That's asking a lot of today's log homes, which, if nothing else, weigh considerably more than frontier cabins. Most log homes today are supported along their horizontal surface to distribute considerable weight throughout logs' length. The more places the logs touch, the more stable the wall is.

This touching occurs two ways. The first is from compression. When the weight of one wall log rests on top of another, individual logs settle onto each other. Cutting a groove can make them fit snugly. Not always, though, because as logs adjust to their new position and location, they move. Whether a little or a lot, movement is inevitable. It's also predictable and controllable. Compression underlies the success of coped and scribe-fit log shapes.

Often, compression isn't sufficient, either because the logs don't weigh enough or the logs are shaped in ways that discourage it. That leads to the second way logs touch. They are cut to fit together, often by precision wood-milling machinery.

Then—and this is the key—the wall logs are held in place so that they work as a unit to withstand wind and seismic forces. It's another of those sum-greater-than-the-parts deals.

Holding wood together requires some kind of nail, screw or bolt. Log construction uses spe-

Fastening logs assures a lasting fit.

cialized versions of these fundamental fasteners. They're usually part of the log-home kit.

▶ **Spikes** are large nails driven into the log.
▶ **Lag screws** are pointed bolts installed in pre-drilled holes in the logs.
▶ **Threaded log-home screws** are smaller in diameter than other fasteners but are heat-treated for equal or greater strength.
▶ **Drift pins** resist lateral loads parallel to the axis of the log. They're set in predrilled holes so that the ends are embedded into the log below.
▶ **Through (or thru) bolts** are connected threaded rods running down through the entire wall. Tightening them during the first year or two takes up any slack caused by settling.

Which fastener works best? They all do the job. By combining human engineering and technology with a naturally sturdy building material, fastening systems ensure that log homes stand steadfast, even under heavy snow and in the face of hurricane-force winds. Put it this way: If Joshua had faced log walls at Jericho, the Bible might have a different ending. ⚘

Know What's in Your Package and What Isn't

20

Understanding how log homes are sold is beneficial. You buy the logs, then you hire someone to assemble them. The log-home kit or materials package is the basic ingredient of your log home.

Packages come in various degrees of completion. When comparing package prices, be sure you know the degree of completion of each package. Generally, there are four types of packages:

Walls Only contains only the logs for the walls, along with fasteners and sealing materials needed to put them together. No roof is supplied, although sometimes log roof beams, doors and windows are included.

Structural Shell includes all that a walls-only package does but adds a roofing system (rafters or trusses) and any roofing system for porches, if any, although perhaps not roof sheathing to cover the rafters or trusses.

Weathertight Shell includes all that a structural shell package does, plus anything needed to keep the weather out, including rough window and door frames, the actual windows and doors, roof sheathing, shingles and all the hardware to fasten everything in place.

Complete Package contains everything that a weathertight shell package contains, but also such indoor components as interior walls, stairs, closet doors, and interior window and door trim. Normally, a complete package does not contain kitchen cabinets, finished flooring, masonry or the utility systems.

There are no industry standards, and each producer comes up with its own variations on these categories. As a result, comparing packages among producers has always been tricky. You would think that you could call three producers, ask for their price on a weathertight shell and choose the least expensive. But it's not as easy as that. Producers have different models, no two exactly alike. Even if you were to ask for the price of a weathertight shell for a home of about 1,800 square feet, you would not be comparing homes that looked exactly alike when finished.

What's more, two producers probably have different notions of "weathertight." Some may supply the hardware for the windows, others don't. Some include the porch stairs, others don't. You have to obtain a detailed materials list before you can compare prices. Even then, you're not really comparing apples to apples. One package might contain pine logs, another cedar. Other variables that can affect the package price are the size of the logs, the degree of pre-cutting, how complicated the log joinery is, preservatives applied before the logs are delivered, whether the logs are kiln-dried, the kind and amount of technical assistance offered, and the quality of blueprints and construction manuals.

In addition, comparing packages requires more than comparing prices. Your preferences in architectural style, log species, windows and doors, hardware, roofing system and roofing materials all come into play. The bottom line is the price of the completed home and your perception of its quality and value.

Whichever package you decide on, the materials that are included in your package constitute a very small portion of the total materials needed to complete your home, at least numerically. Everything that is not in the package, you will have to buy yourself.

There are reasons why some people buy one kind of package and some another. For example, people who buy less than a complete package may have found that they can buy the doors, windows or roof shingles from a local supplier in a style and at a price that they like better than those the producer is offering. People who choose a more complete package may prefer to avoid the hassle of shopping for various components or wish to ensure that all the components are compatible with each other.

The easiest way to compare package prices is get a proposal from one company, then take it to other companies you are considering and let them point out the differences between it and theirs and identify what is missing from the offer you brought to them. You can control the variables to lower your package price, but that doesn't guarantee the final cost of the home will be any different.

It doesn't matter how basic or complete your log package is, you're still going to need the same materials to assemble the finished home. There are a few companies that sell just the logs, period. In fact, any sawmill with the right cutting knives could run you out some logs, probably at a price well below that of the package containing the same kind of

Log homes come in unassembled packages, also called kits.

logs from a full-service log-home company. That's wonderful, but don't for a minute think you'll be saving money. You still have to buy all the sealing and fastening components that even a basic log package contains so the logs will function together as a wall—and you'll be doing this without the benefit of an engineered building system to ensure that the logs are properly set. Any perceived savings would be offset with some, perhaps considerable, risk.

The logs are the biggest item in your log home by volume but represent a mere fraction of the total number of ingredients. A list of materials needed to complete the average log home may run 12 to 15 pages of single-spaced, small-type items. Of those, the log package may constitute only three or four lines. Everything else, you'll need to provide.

The biggest mental obstacle to overcome is that whatever the price of the package may be, it has no bearing on the finished cost of the log home. Yet, when you're shopping for your log home, that's usually the first real number that shows up and is the one you're most likely to remember. Think back to the example (*Chapter 8: Calculate How Much House You Can Afford*) of the Prairie Classic model, how the package price relates to the cost of the home, or rather how it doesn't. What's misleading isn't the dollar amount of the package, it's how you are misled into misinterpreting the information.

Log-home companies often list package price in ads showing a floor plan and photo or rendering of the finished home, prompting your mind to associate that with the package price. The picture you should associate with the package price is two or three tractor-trailers unloading some logs onto the ground at your newly cleared construction site. If you kept that picture in mind, you'd be in a better frame of mind to grapple with the next step: how much money it's going to take to turn that pile of logs into the home pictured in the ad. ❀

"When you pour the concrete slab, put in a pipe for radon mitigation and make sure you have good clean rock under the slab. You may not need it, but it's cheap and easy to put in during construction, but a big pain when the house is all done."

Benshoof Family
Masonville, Colorado

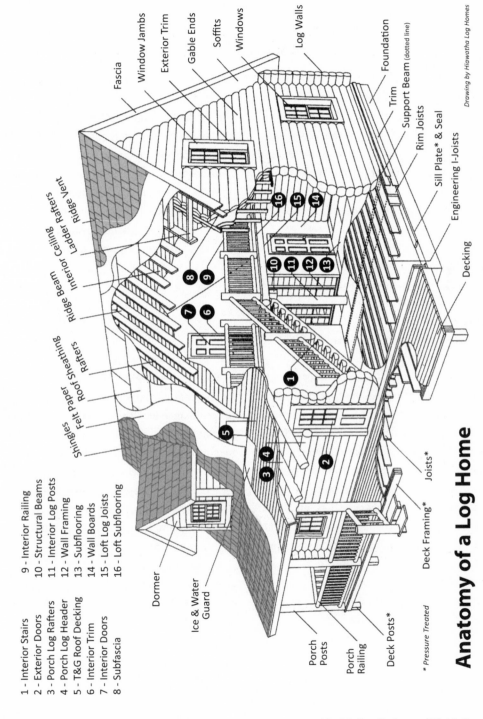

Anatomy of a Log Home

1 - Interior Stairs
2 - Exterior Doors
3 - Porch Log Rafters
4 - Porch Log Header
5 - T&G Roof Decking
6 - Interior Trim
7 - Interior Doors
8 - Subfascia
9 - Interior Railing
10 - Structural Beams
11 - Interior Log Posts
12 - Wall Framing
13 - Subflooring
14 - Wall Boards
15 - Loft Log Joists
16 - Loft Subflooring

Fascia
Window Jambs
Exterior Trim
Gable Ends
Soffits
Windows
Log Walls
Foundation
Trim
Support Beam
Rim Joists
Sill Plate* & Seal
Engineering I-Joists
Decking
Joists*
Deck Framing*
Deck Posts*
Porch Railing
Porch Posts
Ice & Water Guard
Dormer
Shingles
Felt Paper
Sheathing
Roof Rafters
Rafters
Ridge Beam
Interior Ceiling Rafters
Ladder Rafters
Ridge Vent

Drawing by Hiawatha Log Homes

(dotted line)

* Pressure Treated

Passing Grade

Whatever the level of the package you decide is right for you, the common ingredient of all packages is the logs. They must be up to the role they'll play in your home. That means header logs, which span windows and doors, must be able to support greater weight than other wall logs, which are simply stacked one atop the other. But even these logs must be capable of supporting the weight of the house without buckling and causing the roof to sag. How can you be sure the logs you're buying are up to the task?

The best way is to buy logs that are graded for structural performance, as opposed to looks. Structural grading means submitting the logs to a third-party inspection and certification program, which assures that they will perform as specified and that they comply with building codes. Grading applies a uniform standard to a number of conditions (wane, slope of grain, knots, density, insects, decay, shakes, checks, splits, etc.) that affect how the log will behave under stress over time. Evidence of grading is a grade stamp on the logs themselves or a certificate of inspection for each set of logs. The stamp appears on a portion of the log that won't be visible once it becomes part of the home.

The 50-plus companies that belong to the Log Homes Council are required to have their logs graded, either by the council's own grading program or Timber Products Inspection, an independent company. TPI also grades logs for non-LHC members that request its services and can even be hired to grade your logs under its lot-inspection program if the company producing them doesn't grade. Some companies have established their own grading programs, whose standards may or may not exceed those prescribed by the LHC or TPI programs. In addition, many handcrafters don't grade because they usually use the whole log, not sawn portions of logs as most manufacturers do, and don't face the same structural issues.

Buy logs that are graded for structural performance, as opposed to looks.

Both the LHC and TPI train and certify graders and send independent auditors to monitor compliance with the prescribed standards. Companies have to pay for grading and include the cost in their package price.

Both the LHC and TPI programs use different terms for the various grades. For example, the LHC wall-log grades are, from strongest to weakest, Beam, Header, Wall and Utility. TPI uses Premium, Select, Rustic and Wall.

Curiously, log producers often categorize logs by looks. This has nothing to do with grading. Some even offer less visually appealing logs at a cheaper price. Beauty is only skin deep, however, so it's quite possible for less glamorous logs to have a top-quality structural grade. ❀

Understand What a Log Home Costs   21

Folks are forever trying to figure out how much their log home is really, truly going to cost, but the only specific dollar amount you're likely to have in any kind of actual writing is the price for your log package. Even that is usually the amount you saw listed in an ad for one of some company's plans. When has any price in any ad ever been the amount you wind up paying?

Anyway, with this advertised retail log-package price in hand, you present it to anyone who builds or sells log homes for a living and say, "Bottom line it." Maybe you're savvy enough to use the term "turnkey" instead, and in a non-penitentiary way, meaning the cost to build the home to the point where all you have to do is turn the key to the front door and start living the log lifestyle. Since you're committed enough to finding out the answer that you've become involved with salespeople, they might obligingly suggest an answer: magically multiplying the package price (be sure to ask whether to include tax and delivery) by some single digit—digit and a decimal if the salesperson senses you can handle numbers. Times 3, suppose, or 4 (or, to sound even more precise, 3.5).

Here's what's wrong with this line of reasoning. Let's start with: Is that with or without a basement? Finished or unfinished? Or a stud-framed, log-sided second story? Both options involve the same number of log-package parts but obviously a lot more house to build.

Also, look at the different amenities people put in the same-size houses. Cabinets: stock or custom? Countertops: Corian or granite? Fireplace: river rock or manufactured stone? Roofing, flooring and fenestration: designer quality or builder's choice? These are all variables unrelated to the package price. Then there are miscellaneous costs that have nothing to do with the cost of labor and materials, such as permit fees, utility hookups and site preparation, including equipment rental (crane, porta-potty, etc.).

Added to all of these variables is the fact that companies sell different kinds of packages containing different things. Logs, of course, but sometimes a little or much more so. Magic Multiplier or not, even the most complete package isn't going to contain anywhere near what you'll ultimately need. Everything else you'll have to pay for. Suppose you can save $13,000 on a package by buying your own windows and doors, and you can get them yourself for $8,000. Apply your Magic Multiplier to the difference: $15,000

BEFORE: A log shell takes shape on a site in northern Michigan.

or $17,500. A few differences like that could quickly amount to $50,000 or more. On a modest project, that's significant. Even on a grander scale, it isn't small spuds.

The only way you can calculate how many times more your final cost is than the package price is to finish building your log home, then divide the total bill by the package price, either the one you saw advertised or with tax and delivery. But whatever multiplier you then come up with isn't going to be able to predict anyone else's total cost.

Maybe you see from the beginning that the Magic Multiplier isn't going to get the job done. If so, you're probably guessing that the actual numbers to multiply are the square footage of your log home by the cost per square foot to build it. That calculation sounds good in theory, but here's the problem: There's more to buildings than square feet.

Here's one quick example of the square-foot fallacy. A 900-square-foot

AFTER: The finished home fits its site, even featuring roll-down insulated shutters to protect lake-facing windows from bitter winter cold wind off Lake Huron.

building with four walls 30-feet long uses 120 linear feet of wall materials. A second 900-square-foot building with two walls 90 feet long and two walls 10 feet long uses 200 linear feet of wall materials. The result is a 66 percent price difference, based on only one variable.

Now, you aren't likely to build a 90-by-10-foot home, but you see the point? "Generally," says the company whose literature contains the preceding example, "it is the companies appealing to ultra price-sensitive purchasers who will resort to misleading tactics about these kinds of thing." It goes on to advise limiting the importance you place on price per square foot comparisons, stressing, "It is simply not a relevant measure either of materials or labor costs."

"Be careful when signing a time-and-material contract. If you get inexperienced workers they can really run up the cost without any justification."

Benshoof Family
Masonville, Colorado

Here's a probable scenario. Suppose you're looking at a log-home package for a 2,200-square-foot home, and the cost per square foot to build custom homes where you intend building is $175. You conclude that you'll be paying $385,000. That simple calculation overlooks some crucial variables. First are the different levels of complexity in home design. A 2,500-square-foot box is usually less expensive to build than a 2,000-square-foot home with bump-outs, turns, multiple roof pitches and dormers. The building cost can even be affected by such things as site preparation, which has nothing to do with square footage but everything to do with the bottom line.

Next—the level of finish. Hardwood flooring costs more than a subfloor with carpeting, but both materials cover the same square footage. The basic decision as to the size of your logs and whether they are handcrafted or milled will result in different figures. So will whether you act as your own general contractor, hire a dedicated general contractor or hire a multi-project general contractor; the degree of service and quality required; change orders and upgrades once the project is under way; accuracy of bids on labor and materials; and the degree of completion (finishing a basement, for example).

Even if this method had merit, it assumes that every builder building custom homes within a defined geographical territory is charging the same cost per square foot. First, the cost per square foot anywhere is an average of all similar projects; some homes cost more, others less. Plus, builders compete for projects. After you realize that costs do differ from builder to builder, you ask for bids. Some quote a lower cost per square foot than the average. These low-ballers rarely pass along any savings to you, however. More likely, they'll lower the quality of the finishes, fixtures, appliances, interior doors and mechanical systems they provide to keep their profit margin steady. Sometimes a tad, other times a lot.

Builder-grade is something to sneer at, even in starter homes, which your log home certainly won't be. "Builders concentrate their energy where their buyers will compare—generally the kitchen, the master bathroom, bedroom count and overall square footage," Ron Jones, editor of *Green Builder* magazine, told syndicated columnist Katherine Salant. "For those things least familiar to consumers, a builder takes the path of least resistance and installs the bare minimum in performance and warranty."

For example, Jones points out, a builder might choose appliances whose brand the buyer recognizes but provide cheaper models in the line. For items such as windows, a builder will use a no-name brand. In terms of useful life, Jones cautions, "if the standard of the home-builder industry for a particular item is five years and it is not a selling point for buyers, there's not much incentive to offer a longer one."

Then there are the amenities. The decision to have a fireplace alone could radically affect the cost to build a home without changing the square footage. Same with a Jacuzzi tub or a priceless antique chandelier.

The biggest variable is the quality of the builder. If every builder charges the same cost per square foot, rest assured that mediocre builders are benefiting more than the super-duper ones. They have no incentive to work their hardest or do their best.

The good news is that builders who specialize in log construction often are proud of their special niche and go out of their way to help buyers and guide them to better choices. They aren't sacrificing their profit, by any means, but they operate on the assumption that log-home buyers expect better than slack-off labor and builder-grade features.

As with everything else involved in buying and building a log home, there are no shortcuts when it comes to figuring the cost. The only way you can reasonably *estimate* the total is to get bids on the materials and labor involved. The process will take time and effort, but the result will be numbers that reflect actual reality.

And your only chance of ever knowing the true cost of your log home is to sit down after you've moved in and add up everything. If you want to entertain yourself by determining the cost per square foot or the ratio of the finished cost to the package price, go ahead. Just realize that whatever you come up with, that's no guarantee that you could turn right around and build an identical home in the same location for the same price.

Start with a detailed cost estimate based on actual bids for every single item that will go into your log home.

If 20 years of writing about log homes and talking with log-home owners have taught me anything, it is that there are no easy answers. You're asking for trouble if you think there are, or if you believe someone who assures you otherwise. What's more important is to take the time to get everything right, starting with a detailed cost estimate based on bids for every single item that will go into your log home and the labor required for the home's assembly.

Crunching these numbers will prove to be a formidable task, but it's the only way to get a true picture. Don't let yourself be misled along the way so that you wind up shortchanging yourself in the long run. Not having enough money to cover the true cost, whatever it turns out to be, can delay or scuttle your project. Be prepared.

But if you're the sort of person who needs a carrot on a stick to persevere through this cost-estimating process, here's the good news. Once the home is built, its value, due to what comparable neighboring homes are selling for, is determined by other factors than your labor and materials costs. Add to that fiduciary benefit the ultimate curb appeal of logs, both for looks and sturdiness, and your log home probably will be worth at or near the top— unless you're in a community with other log homes.

Get to Know Your Dealer   22

Log-home companies are spread all over North America. That doesn't mean you can't or shouldn't deal with them. In fact, very few log homes are built in the shadow of the mills and yards where the logs are produced. Many companies have sales representatives, usually called dealers, sometimes builder-dealers, who work in assigned territories. As you search for companies to produce your log home, you'll likely find yourself talking to a dealer covering the area where you intend to build your log home.

Twenty years ago, when building log homes was evolving from a curiosity into the mainstream, producers enlisted some of their customers to be sales representatives. These people used their own homes as models for the producer. Potential customers might visit the home, like it and sign up to buy one from the company. The representative who showed the home took the order and received a commission. These early dealers for the log-home industry generally worked part time. Many dealers today operate this way, although many more regard selling log homes as a full-time career and provide additional, specialized services, plus travel to their companies' plants for training in sales and construction design.

These dealers can help you immensely because they know their territory, and they know log homes and what it takes to get one built, if for no other reason than that they've sold homes in their area that have been built and are now lived in. A good dealer can help you find land. By acting as your liaison with your log-home company, your dealer can help you design your home by coordinating with the company's in-house designers and by knowing the prevailing style of log home in the area. Your dealer can help you find financing, again by knowing who has financed the homes the dealer has sold, as well as other log homes in the area that competing dealers have sold. For this same reason, your dealer can help you find a builder by recommending one or more who have built log homes in the area, including those from the company the dealer is representing. Some dealers provide log-home construction services, hence the term builder-dealer.

Many builder-dealers keep their construction business separate from the sales function. You sign two contracts: one for the purchase of the log home and a second to build and finish the home. One payment goes to the log-home company, the other to the dealer's construction company.

Even if the representative with whom you are working is a builder-dealer, you are under no obligation to use the construction service just because you buy the home from that person. You may decide, however, to include bids from builder-dealers with those from other builders.

A few companies don't use dealers but have sales representatives that work out of the national or a regional office. They provide the same services as dealers but are employees of the company.

It is important that you understand the relationship between any dealer you talk to and the producer that he or she represents. Some relationships are close, others loose.

The critical point comes when you are asked to make a deposit. Your money might go to the dealer, or it might pass through the dealer, who gives it to the producer. Dealers sometimes represent more than one log-home company. Some, when they take your order for a log home, may actually buy the log-home package wholesale and resell it to you retail.

Just as you will check out everyone whose services you use throughout the process of buying and building your log home, you will want to assure yourself that the sales representative handling your transaction is reputable and reliable.

▶ Check the dealer's professional reputation. If you're satisfied with the reliability of the producer, its dealer is also likely to be reputable. But it never hurts to check with local business organizations.

▶ Find out the dealers' relationship with the producer. Does the dealer work for the producer you are considering or represent it exclusively? Or is the dealer an agent for several companies or one who buys and re-sells homes? Know who's taking responsibility before you make a down payment.

▶ If your dealer will also be your builder, learn how good a builder the dealer is. Are previous customers satisfied? Has the dealer built enough homes to count as experienced? Has she completed training courses with the producer? Does he meet deadlines? Are his workers agreeable? Does she return phone calls promptly?

At some point, the log-home company may ask about your interest in becoming one of its dealers, especially if the dealer you're working with has too big a territory or is looking to sever its relationship with the company (or vice-versa). It is even likelier that you may express interest in becoming a dealer. It is a great second career if you really like log homes, enjoy meeting other people who like them and want to help them toward their goal of living in one. It's also a fun job for couples who enjoy working together and want to work out of their log home.

Most companies want dealers who work full time and regard the job as a business, not a hobby, however. And none will give you a free log home on your promise of becoming a dealer. Build your home first and then inquire about dealer opportunities.

Companies are always on the lookout for dealers. A few, though, are in the business of selling dealerships. Be wary of any log-home company that encourages you to become a dealer even before you've bought or built a home, especially if it asks you to put up any money.

If you are genuinely interested in selling log homes for a living, ask about your dealer's relationship with the log-home company. Talk to other dealers. Many companies have recruitment portfolios to show prospective dealers. Ask for one. Also, ask the company if you can attend its next dealer meeting. ❀

Get Answers Before You Buy

John Kupferer's original *Log Home Magazine Annual Buyer's Guide* had a cornball log logo, but it was packed with essential information that helped the first generation of log-home buyers understand the steps involved. A mainstay of these 300-page guides was "25 Questions to Ask Before You Buy." These questions informed buyers what to find out from salespeople's presentations and log-home companies' sales literature. I'm reprinting a shortened version you can use as a checklist. Make sure you cover all these points when interviewing log home companies.

○ Are you satisfied you're dealing with reputable people?

○ Do you fully understand the terms of the purchase contract?

○ Do you know what your package includes and what it doesn't?

○ Do you know the quality of the components being provided?

○ What wood species will your logs be?

○ Will the logs be green, air dried, kiln dried or standing dead?

○ Will the logs in your package be completely pre-cut, partially pre-cut or linear footage?

○ Will your logs be treated with a preservative before they're delivered?

○ Will the producer provide an itemized cost of the package?

○ Have you obtained competitive bids on the package from two or more companies?

○ Do you understand the cost and conditions of delivery of your package?

○ Will your logs be graded?

○ Will the home meet local building codes?

○ Does the producer provide on-site technical assistance?

○ Has someone explained the technical aspect of the producer's building system in layperson's terms?

○ Does the producer offer custom-design service?

○ What services will your company sales rep provide?

Visit Several Actual Log Homes by Your Producer and Builder

23

Everything about the log-home company and the builder you're think-ing about hiring may strike you as fantastic. Good people, nice sales literature or web site, professional-looking pickup truck, custom-made hardhat—these are all great. Maybe you've inspected the company's logs or even visited the mill. Looks like a go, but wait. How do you know the homes stand up and hold up well or that the builder understands the concepts of level and plumb? Don't just check out references or see pictures of the work. Inspect actual homes built from the company's logs according to its building system and the workmanship of your builder.

I'll never forget the first time a log-home company invited me to visit its new sales model. I had met some of the company officials, even interviewed some owners of its homes for features in my magazine, but this was going to be my first look at an actual log home. I drove into the parking lot with great anticipation. Several friendly employees were on hand to greet me. The place looked great. Not too big or showy, but homey. I looked around and then started noticing the details. There were small gaps between some of the logs, even though the home was only a few months old. I thought that if this is the example of its product that it wants to show off, what must its regular homes turn out like? I had the opportunity not long after to visit some of its actual homes. The owners seemed satisfied with them, but I detected plenty of flaws in the logs and the workmanship. One owner raved about the home while admitting she was disappointed with the way it turned out and with the company she bought it from. I asked why she praised a home she didn't like. "Because I thought I could persuade you to show it in your magazine to help me sell it," she admitted. Even though the company was a steady advertiser in my magazine, I wouldn't feature one of its homes. It eventually went out of business.

You owe it to yourself before buying any log home to have a good idea how it's going to turn out. Look at homes at least five years old, and try to talk to the owners without the log-home company dealer or the builder present. If you're at a loss as to what to look for, hire a log-home consultant to accompany you. There are such services, although most of the ones advertising their services turn out to be working for log-home companies. That isn't necessarily a bad thing because you know they'll really scrutinize a competitor's work. An engineer with experience evaluating log structures is a better judge.

I recommend concentrating on the fit of the logs, not just along their length, but also at the corners and where they intersect door and window frames. Anything that doesn't align or isn't level raises suspicion. Look for

any patching or gaps. Basically, any evidence that the building system failed to accommodate log movement as the home settled is cause for concern.

A reason for inspecting homes with the owners present but not the log-home company representatives is that you can ask a lot of questions and get candid answers. You know the owners are generally satisfied with their home or else the companies wouldn't be using them as references, but sometimes comments or even small gripes can be telling.

"The logs were delivered on time, but a few were missing, and we had to wait for them to come along, which they did just a day or two later."

"The company wasn't happy when I told them I wanted to buy my own windows, and they kept warning me that they couldn't be responsible if they didn't fit right. The builder and the window company assured me they'd work, and they did, but I didn't appreciate the log-home company pressuring me."

As far as checking out builders, see the next chapter (*Hire the Best Builder—not the Cheapest*) for general criteria, but again, as you inspect the work, ask questions about what the builder was like to work with: Did the crew clean up the site every night or leave it a mess? If you could do it all again, what's one thing you'd do differently? Why did you like this builder? Perhaps the homeowner's answer to the last question is that it was because the builder handled all the decisions—"so we didn't have to worry about anything." That's praise indeed, but suppose you're a hands-on kind of person who wants to be involved in every detail, to the point that you'll probably try your builder's patience, but you don't care. A take-charge builder might not suit you.

Perhaps it matters a lot to you that as your home is going up, no one smokes anywhere near it, especially inside. Whatever your preferences are, make sure you find a builder that will listen to you, comply with your instructions and accept that you're the boss.

To get back to the log-home companies, everyone wishes there were a consumer rating of companies so that you could be sure you were dealing with the best one, not the third or fourth best. Unlike appliances, no publication or consumer panel rates the companies because of the subjective nature of these businesses. You ought to realize by now that the variables among companies and their products are so vast as for any rating to be unreliable for making your choice.

Metal roofs are a pop topping for log homes.

If you want some measure of assurance that at least the company is trustworthy, however, there are two organizations whose members subscribe to quality standards and ethical business practices:

The Log Homes Council
800-368-5242
www.loghomes.org
(over 50 U.S. members, all manufacturers)

International Log Builders Association
www.logassociation.org
(72 North American members, mostly handcrafters)

Hire the Best Builder, Not the Cheapest

24

Building is the most crucial part of the whole process. This should be obvious by the fact that your log home comes unassembled and must be put together according to detailed instructions to fulfill the requirements of the log producer's engineered building system. Finding a competent builder isn't always easy, especially when you're building your home in a sparsely populated area where craftmanship doesn't abound.

Maybe there are one or two builders known far and wide for their quality work and talented crews. They're so good, in fact, that they can't schedule your project for at least another year. Meanwhile, six or seven builders are available to start tomorrow. You don't know anything about them, but the mere fact that they're available and eager to get going ought to make you at least a little skeptical of their ability.

A good log-home builder is worth paying and waiting for. A bad builder can waste your time and money, and ruin the best-designed, best-engineered home.

The few complaints I've heard against log-home companies turned out to be the fault of builders who didn't build the home the way it was supposed to be built, perhaps through negligence or perhaps through carelessness. Remember, by the time your builder goes to work, the log producer is out of the picture, except for technical assistance the builder has to request—and not be too proud to request it. No one is making sure the builder is following the detailed instructions. You have to take it on faith.

Builders sometimes offer to save you money (or cut their own costs) by compromising the system. The log producer may specify that each log needs two beads of caulk, one on the inside, the other on the outside. Your builder figures to cut the cost of caulking in half by applying only one bead of caulk, on the inside of the log, where it will prevent any rain or wind from coming inside. As it happens, the caulking does its job, but only until wind and rain coming through the space between the logs break the seal and begin infiltrating your living space. By this time, unfortunately, enough moisture has collected between the logs, thanks to no outer bead of caulk to keep it out, that rot has already begun and in a place that is virtually impossible to inspect and prohibitively expensive to repair.

Handcrafters stack their logs and then use chain saws to cut out window openings on the site. The task requires skill and a sure hand since a mistake could prove costly.

Building a log home isn't all that different from building an ordinary home—except for the logs. And these are mostly the walls and often just the perimeter walls. All the stuff on top of the walls and inside the walls is pretty much the same as any house. There isn't log-home plumbing and log-home refrigerators and log-home flooring and log-home closets. So once you've gotten the walls taken care of, the rest isn't that big of a mystery. Some elements require planning, especially plumbing and wiring.

The builder is the person you will trust to assemble and finish your log home. You want one who'll build it right. It may be your dealer; if not, find the best one available that you can afford.

▶ **If you can't find a builder yourself, ask your dealer for referrals.**
Dealers who aren't also builders know builders who've satisfactorily built the homes the dealers sold.

- ▶ **Check the builder's licenses.** Make sure they're up to date and that the builder has workmen's compensation and liability insurance.
- ▶ **Ask about the builder's reputation.** Check with local business and builders associations. Also, get referrals from previous customers.
- ▶ **Choose a builder that communicates easily.** Builders should be able to explain what's going on, be open to your suggestions, welcome you to the construction site.
- ▶ **As a rule, hire a builder who has built log homes—and inspect these homes.** Look for a builder with experience not just building log homes, but also with your log-home type of construction and with the size and scope of your log home. All log homes are not built alike.

Is log-building experience essential? No, but consider whether you want someone learning on your home.

Because having to find their own builder discourages many potential homebuyers, more log-home companies are teaming up with builders and training them to build the companies' homes to completion. In some cases, companies are setting up their own construction services, although perhaps limited to a certain distance from their home base because of the expense of sending crews far afield. In both cases, you gain assurance that your home will be assembled correctly, and you still have the opportunity to hire your own crew to take care of the finishing steps.

Once you've chosen your builder, taking the following steps can smooth the construction of your log home.

Get everything in writing. If the

Setting a ridge beam with the crane.

builder says something will be done, get that assurance on paper. Rather than ask the builder to draw up some contractual document that hints of litigation, you can just jot down things you would like done or changed and then get the builder to initial or sign after every item. Make two copies: one for you, the other for your builder. If there's a cost involved, list that and have it signed or initialed, too.

Keep a chronological record of conversations involving your project, showing time and date. It'll help with follow-up and to resolve issues. Calling someone and saying you spoke with someone a few weeks ago who promised to deliver such-and-such, you'll get better response by saying, "I called on October 5 at 3:15 and spoke with Mr. Flood, who said he'd deliver the such-and-such by noon yesterday. I followed up the day before yesterday, and Mr. Jenkins said he'd remind Mr. Flood about the delivery. I'm calling because the delivery wasn't made and I'd like to know why and when I can expect the such-and-such."

Keep on top of things. Visit the site as often as you can, ideally at the beginning or the end of the workday. Show an interest in the work,

compliment good workmanship and discuss any decisions you need to make, such as the specific location of fixtures, outlets and switches. Speak up when something displeases you and when something promised hasn't happened.

Schedule a more formal meeting with the builder at least once a month to review progress and see how your instructions are being carried out. Make sure you have your notes on hand to refer to. Point out anything that needs to be corrected and discuss specific plans for the upcoming month.

Be friendly but not too palsy-walsy. The builder is working for you and doesn't need to know about your personal life. You might offer to fetch lunch for the crew (better yet, deliver a home-made one) or even stop by with a six-pack for the end of the workweek to toast a job well done, but keep your distance. When the home is finished, you might want to throw a party for everyone involved. If it's a large group, have it catered (the food doesn't need to be fancy), maybe provide some live entertainment. Invite the workers' families, too, so they can share in the pride and welcome you to their community. ❀

Overhead views reveal the complexity of log construction as the wall logs are stacked (opposite page) and then the gable logs and trusses are set in place with the purlins that will support the roof.

25 Determine Your Level of Involvement

The prospect of owning a log home has the capacity to awaken a trail-blazing tendency, even in the most armchair-anchored urbanite. If you feel yourself so moved, recall this snippet of dialog from TV's "Seinfeld":

George: We could build a cabin like (snaps fingers) that.

Jerry: Well, maybe not us, but two men could.

Building a log cabin, let alone a log home, is hardly a project to undertake on a whim. At the same time, it is an understandable ambition. Few people think about buying a log home without wondering whether they could and should contribute their labor to shape the outcome.

People commonly cite three reasons for intending to get involved in building their log home: for the experience, the sense of accomplishment or the savings. Any or all may be encouraging you to consider playing a leading or supporting role in your project. No matter how noble your motives or firm your commitment may seem, be honest with yourself about your ability to tackle and complete such an undertaking.

Perhaps longing for hands-on lies at the root of why you wanted a log home in the first place. After all, log homes began as the ultimate do-it-yourself project. You built one or else. As they evolved from frontier cabins to full-fledged houses, however, the handcrafting skills required to make them became more specialized, ultimately producing the grand lodges of the West and the Great Camps of the Adirondacks.

These triumphs inspired everyday middle-class people from the 1930s on to build their own vacation cabins. Even so, not many folks grabbed a trusty ax and headed off to the woods to chop down the trees they needed. Getaway cabins of this era came in pre-cut kits. They required little skill to assemble because few people considered them anything but makeshift. They rarely included any amenities and were usually used seasonally when weather permitted, mostly in the summer. Some were built as hunting camps with perhaps a wood-burning stove or a huddle-around fireplace.

Today, almost nine out of ten log homes are people's permanent residence. They aren't all that much trickier to build than ordinary stick-framed houses, but they do require considerable expertise. These aren't weekend cabins in the woods. They're full-blown, up-to-date homes with all the systems and features capable of supporting the life you already have or aspire to, including all the space, all the gadgetry and all the amenities.

Let me put it bluntly: If you aren't equipped to build an ordinary house, you're unlikely to build a log home.

When determining your involvement, assess not just your skill, but also your degree of commitment. Unless you're retired or taking a year or more off from work to devote your full time and attention to the project, you'll be working on it evenings and weekends—essentially part time. That means the whole job could easily take two years or longer. That's a sacrifice few people are willing to make, even if they're capable.

Although the work is hard and time-consuming, it may be worthwhile if you anticipate the experience will be spiritually or financially rewarding. Never, however, base your decision solely on how much money you figure to save. If you can't afford to begin the project at your present skill level, acquire either more money or greater skill. Thinking you can build

> "I intended being my own general contractor. When the logs were delivered and we were ready for the framing crew to stack them, nobody showed up. We were sitting here with logs everywhere. I also had trouble keeping subs because they're so busy out here. That's probably why I ended up doing so much more work than I had planned."
>
> Palmer Family
> Loveland, Colorado

a log home yourself just because you can't afford to do it any other way will most likely result in a home that is disappointing.

I'll never forget the homeowner who delighted in showing me the many details he had incorporated into his magnificent home. Everything was perfect, and he was justifiably proud. When I asked if he saved money by doing any of the construction work himself, he turned to me and declared unabashedly, "Sir, I saved money by doing none of the work myself!" He knew his limitations and had hired experienced experts to do the work he couldn't but knew needed doing.

If you aren't handy with tools, maybe you aspire to be your own general contractor. How hard could that be? The shelves of bookstores and home-improvement centers are lined with guides to being your own general contractor, all of them promising you'll save in the neighborhood of 25 percent on your project. But even that work takes time, is detail oriented and may not save as much as you think.

First, you'll need to be on the job most every day. Again, if you're holding down a full-time job (a likely circumstance if you're expecting to qualify to borrow money to finance the purchase and construction of your log home), you'll be giving up most of your free time supervising others, scheduling work, arranging deliveries and trouble-shooting.

Second, you'll be hiring a builder and subcontractors to do the actual work. Most likely, the pool of workers will come from a rural area where you know no one and no one knows you. Be wary of those who promise to

> "We wanted to save money by peeling the logs ourselves. I managed to hand-peel two with a drawknife. That job is much harder than it looks. After completing just the two, my back went out, and we decided it was time to hire the professionals."
>
> Schmidt Family
> Wilson, Wyoming

Building a log home requires attention to details that go beyond the stacked-log walls.

possess construction skills. That's not to say there aren't many talented, ingenious tradespeople, even in remote areas. Most, if they are any good, are gainfully employed by a full-time, licensed contractor, and few are likely to abandon that relationship and steady work to tackle your one-time project. That means the subs most likely to work for you are the ones no one else but you will hire.

Third, your savings may be illusory. A full-time contractor can probably get a better price than you on materials, not just by knowing where to shop, but also by buying in sufficient quantities to get a discount. And you may need to buy or lease a pickup truck. People in cities and suburbs drive pickups more for status than practicality, but on construction jobs they're not for showing off. Being a general contractor means running a lot of errands and hauling a lot of supplies and not getting stuck in the mud that characterizes construction sites.

Consider, too, that intending to be your own builder or the general contractor lumps you into the category of owner-builder. Few lenders are willing to advance money to inexperienced people. The reason is simple. Until your house is actually built, it isn't worth much more than a pile of logs and some other materials sitting on the ground. The money you hope to borrow is based on the amount the home will be worth if you default and the lender has to sell the property to recoup its investment. A built home has value. A pile of logs, even if they're nicely stacked and neatly covered, is of no use to a banker.

If you have proven building experience or a contractor's license, then you might be able to find a bank to back your venture. Otherwise, scale

Setting an entry truss.

"I worked on every inch of my house myself except the concrete and drywall, and exercised diligently at a health club for a year prior to starting to prepare myself for lifting wall logs and rafters."

Sumner Family
Bellbrook, Ohio

down your ambitions. Your best opportunity for sweat equity is handling labor-intensive tasks that require little skill, most notably sanding and staining your logs. When you are on the job site, offer to run errands, especially to bring lunch for the crew. Help clean up after the day's work. It'll give you a chance to inspect the work without appearing to be checking up on the crew and will make them more willing to accept your suggestions. Because they're also long-standing members of the community you're moving to, they're likelier to spread the word that you're a good egg.

By the same token, if you do go ahead and assume general contractor's duties, try to set up temporary quarters on the site. Some homeowners build a guesthouse first to work from; others sleep in a camper or RV.

Even if you contribute nothing physically to the completion of your home, you will be asked to make dozens of decisions as the work progresses. That's more than enough involvement for most people.

You can take part another way. Start a journal, blog or Twitter to record and share your experience. Take pictures to supplement your narrative. Go beyond the actual details of construction. Record discoveries about your new area: shopping, restaurants, neighbors, recreation, wildlife, services and tradespeople (yes, some subs who won't work for you if you're a general contractor will be happy to help out with weekend handyman projects for extra money—and you'll already know their capabilities and dependability).

Also, while your home is being built is a good time to be shopping for furniture and accessories. Many homeowners prefer to hire local artists and craftspeople to create special pieces. Getting them started before the house is done will allow them to feel part of the creative process and also work with the builder if there'll be any special installation requirements. ❀

"I wanted to build our home myself because that was about the only way we could afford to do it. But I was still working full time and found that even when I could be at the site all day, with it just being me, I wasn't getting anything done. I called our sales rep, who referred me to a young builder who brought along some friends and his cousin to help him. Boy, things just started taking off. My nephew came to do the electrical. My son and wife helped, along with anybody we could get. It turned out to be kind of a community project."

Carter Family
Pataskala, Ohio

Still Determined?

If you weigh the pros and cons and still relish the opportunity to build your log home yourself—and from scratch yet—there are schools that teach log building. To find a directory of log and timber building schools, check out *www.logassociation.org/directory/schools.php*. Individually, the better known (and current at the time this book was published) are:

Arbor Vitae Log Craft
www.arborvitaelogcraft.com

Great Lakes School of Log Building
www.schooloflogbuilding.com

Lasko School of Log Building, Inc.
www.laskoschooloflogbuilding.com

Log Home Builders
www.logbuilders.org

Logworks School
www.logworksschool.com

Montana School of Log Building
http://cu.imt.net/~logworker/

Moose Mountain Log Home Course
www.moosemountain.com

Norwegian School of Log Building
www.norsklafteskole.no

Pat Wolfe's Log Building School
www.logbuildingschool.net

Rocky Mountain Workshops
www.rockymountainworkshops.com

Some log-home manufacturers offer hands-on workshops that won't teach you how to stack your logs but will acquaint you with the task, and you may find a log handcrafter willing to take you on as a sub-apprentice. Even a series of carpentry classes—from beginner to at least intermediate, preferably advanced—at your local vocational school will allow you to tackle some of the finish work. My neighbor learned how to drive a Bobcat and handled a lot of the pre-construction and post-construction site work.

Students at Moose Mountain's three-week log-building course.

How-To Books

Books can give you an idea of what it takes and give you a measure of confidence:

Log Construction Manual: The Ultimate Guide to Building Handcrafted Log Homes by Robert Chambers (Deep Stream Press, 272 pages, $37.95) is that rare volume whose title understates its contents. It really does teach log building. If the price seems steep for a book, consider it cheap for a course covering in detail everything you'll need to know to build your home. Be forewarned, though, that, like any school, there's math involved. Fortunately, it's practical, not theoretical.

The book opens with an overview of the advantages of log construction, then progresses step by step through the entire process of building a scribe-fit, handcrafted home. Highlights along the way are the author's "Log Selection Rules," aimed at turning logs into walls efficiently; cutting notches, saddles and grooves; settling, including a settling quiz (more math); and log-building tools. The chapter on tools is worth the price of tuition, especially the two pages devoted to where to buy them.

Beyond guiding the person who's intent on building a log home, the book's value is the realistic picture its author portrays. It allows anyone contemplating the task to evaluate what's involved, then determine whether to proceed or turn the job over to a pro. It's worth keeping in mind this assessment from the author: "The basics skills of scribing and cutting can be learned in short order—perhaps just a few days. But handcrafted log construction is not easy—it requires practice, time, effort and patience."

If it seems like too much, better to bail out after reading the book than when you're knee deep in logs and debt. If you do abandon the project, or even if you have no illusions about undertaking it in the first place, the *Log Construction Manual* offers a fascinating chronicle that can only deepen your appreciation of what's involved in building one of these splendid homes, even when the builder is a seasoned pro.

B. Allan Mackie looms as a legend among the current generation of log builders, many of whom learned their craft from him or his original students. Mackie can rightly be called the father of today's log building. Not to pay him heed is folly.

Many years have elapsed since Mackie's seminal work, *Building with Logs*, set down clearly a systematic approach to log construction, clearly written and brimming with wisdom. In 1997, Firefly Books issued an eighth, revised edition of the 1971 original. The lessons and advice still rang true, but the intervening 26 years had seen an almost total transformation of log homes, from a cottage trade to a billion-dollar industry. As a result, *Building with Logs* seemed too quaint to be taken practically.

Fortunately, Mackie has remained in touch with the times. He issued his updated ideas in *The Owner-Built Home: Living in Harmony with Your Environment* (Firefly Books, 232 pages, $24.95). Like its predecessor, it lays out the entire experience of building a log home, beginning with the trees and winding up with the finishing touches, which define the character of individual homes.

Mackie delves beyond the practical side, however, revealing his passion for the craft. Attitude, he believes, is as important as carpentry skills. "When the builder and the tree understand what is needed, they work together in harmony, each aiding the other," he writes in the first chapter, "The Purpose in Building a Log House." Such sentiments merit reading not just by anyone thinking about building a log home, but also by everyone thinking about living in one. "You'll know very early," he explains, "that the real reason you need a log house is to heal and strengthen your soul by providing a true place for your heart to touch (ever so gently) nature, to which we are all connected."

Both Mackie and Chambers recognize that there's more to log homes than the wood. This understanding shines through both books.

For those interested in building a log home and incorporating solar and wind energy, *Crafting Log Homes Solar Style: An Inspiring Guide to Self-Sufficiency* by Rex & LaVonne Ewing (PixyJack Press, 256 pages, $25) provides a healthy dose of how-to log construction combined with the modern technology of renewable energy.

How-to books can give you an idea of what it takes and give you a measure of confidence.

These three volumes are the tip of a logjam, if you will. Others are contemporary, but many are reprints of bygone classics (read: copyright free), appeal to nostalgia and are entertaining diversions, even if never used to undertake a log-building project. Among my favorites are:

Little Book of Log Cabins: How to Build and Furnish Them by William S. Wicks (originally published in 1920, available as a Dover reprint, $6.95 paperback).

How to Build and Furnish a Log Cabin: The Easy, Natural Way Using Only Hand Tools and the Woods Around You by W. Ben Hunt ($12.95 paperback), which combines two books: Building a Log Cabin (1947) and Rustic Construction (1939).

How to Build Your Dream Cabin in the Woods: The Ultimate Guide to Building and Maintaining a Backcountry Getaway by J. Wayne Fears ($14.95, paperback). The author of this 2002 how-to book not only promises that such a cabin can be yours at a price that won't break the bank, he also delivers.

Log Cabins and How to Build Them by William Swanson (originally published 1948, reprinted as a Lyons Press paperback 2001; out of print but used copies plentiful, starting at around $10). ❀

26 Expect Delays

Spring rains filled the footings excavation.

Don't schedule a big party for the day after your builder promises your home will be ready. It's a rare log home that gets built on time. Rare enough that I've never heard of it happening. Oh, homeowners may start out saying the builder beat the deadline, which invariably is a major family get-together, usually a holiday. But then they add something along the lines of, "After our company left, the builder did have to come back and finish a few details." Like hang the bathroom doors.

That's close enough for a cigar, but usually builders miss the mark by enough to really aggravate their clients. The notoriety of such occurrences is why so many people building a log home—or any custom home, for that matter—begin the entire project, back around Chapter 7, with utter dread. Some homeowners have fired builders in mid project for taking too long. Other builders are so derelict that your only recourse is legal action.

But consider this. It's difficult to forecast a specific completion date before the project even begins.

A major storm or a late delivery can result in a few days' setback that can never be made up. And builders don't like delays any more than you do, especially if they have another job lined up they're eager to get started. Builders usually get paid by the job, but their crew gets paid for the time they're on the job.

You certainly don't want the job to drag on way beyond your target date, but you'll gain little by pressuring your builder to hurry up. In the rush to meet the deadline, the builder might cut a few corners or not live up to the standards of the rest of the work. More important than getting your home done is getting it done right.

Be flexible and understanding. Instead of viewing your builder's inevitable delay as yet one more reason to be aggravated, regard it as an opportunity to use the extra time to shop for new furniture. ❀

"Our delays included the foundation guy never showing up, record-breaking spring rains, the well driller getting stuck on our new road, several heavy snowstorms in the fall, and the electrician not finishing the job. Building our own home was a character-building experience, to say the least, but one we are proud of."

Ewing Family
Masonville, Colorado

Only a foot of snow to shovel out of the house this time.

27 Don't Forget Furniture

Allow money in your budget for the finishing touches. A picture-perfect setting and matching interior are what log homes are all about. Nothing's more disappointing than a brand-new home with worn-out furniture and an outside that looks like construction is still under way.

As monumental an accomplishment as building a log home is, it is but the prelude to why you wanted a log home in the first place—to live in. It isn't finished until it's furnished. A log home is a stage that must be set.

By the time you are ready to move in, you should already have some idea of how to proceed with this next, exciting phase. Now is not the time to begin thinking of decorating your home. It's best to begin thinking about furniture and accessories even before you rough out ideas for the home's design and then think about it throughout the process. Many homeowners acquire pieces along the way and store them until they're ready to move into place—a reason why some people build the garage first and then the house.

Furnishing a log home is a challenge for most people because the space is so different from just about anything you've experienced before. Unlike walls in conventional houses, log walls are not a neutral element. They impose color and texture. Also, if your home follows the trend of other log homes, the rooms will be bigger than you're accustomed to, if not in terms of square footage, then surely of volume. Finally, there's the whole issue of which styles are appropriate for a log home—and which aren't.

Furnish your log home to reflect your personality and accommodate your lifestyle. You will never feel comfortable in a home that is out of character with how you live. You must be true to your taste.

The first step, therefore, is to identify just what you aspire to. This should be done with some sense of ensemble. That is, you should have a coherent vision of what you want individual rooms and the rooms all together to look like, even before you acquire the furniture to place in them.

Fortunately, if you are among those who don't know what you like until you see it, visual references are plentiful. The pages of log-home magazines abound with color photographs showing furniture in actual log homes. Save those showing groupings or individual pieces to your liking, just as you did images of homes to spark your structural design ideas.

A sure-fire way to organize furnishings is by theme. You don't have to resort to clichés and conventions, but themes are an excellent starting point. Here are some of the more familiar themes popular among log-home owners.

Country is the predominant style, no doubt because it hearkens back to simpler times. It is also the most versatile. The term "country" takes in a range of subcategories: farmhouse, mountain, cowboy, Southwest and down-home. These motifs can range from quaint to hokey, but the overriding characteristics are informality and comfort. Handcrafted antique furniture is the cornerstone of country decor, ranging from classic stylings to primitive pieces, although the hallmark of true country is its timelessness.

French Country is a popular variation. Its trademarks are yellows, blues, rooster collections and tiles on the floor and kitchen walls. When applied to interior design, it generally means a mix between elegant and rustic. Faded or whitewashed wood, blue, pink and yellow small prints and flowered fabrics, sunflowers in a dripware pitcher are elements that constitute French Country.

Cottage Country is popular among log homes used as summer getaways. This style features an interesting variety of pastel colors in floral- or fruit-patterned fabrics. Painted wicker furniture is common.

Rustic is the most primitive country style. In fact, the term is often used interchangeably with country. Rustic furniture is made from tree branches and trunks, usually with the bark left on. Items in this category include bearskin rugs, antique snowshoes, old woodsman's and farm tools, oil lamps hanging on the wall and any other handcrafted antique items.

Cabin Chic centers on homespun and primitive items intended to re-create the log cabin of the American myth. This is usually a theme confined to one portion of the house. It is especially appropriate in restored cabins of the 18th and 19th centuries. Collectibles are the foundations of this style, which is certainly the most whimsical.

Western takes in a broad range, although wood furniture, painted or unpainted, is central. Hand-forged metal and elk-horn chandeliers are common accessories. The passion for the cowboy look centers on the dude-ranch creations of Thomas Molesworth and his followers that evoke the romance of the Wild West. Bright colors, particularly blues and reds, dominate the fabrics. Another distinctive trademark of Molesworth furniture is burled wood, which is common in the lodgepole-pine forests around Jackson Hole and Cody, Wyoming, where the style first flourished.

Southwestern is inspired by the desert, but is unexpectedly at home with logs. Adobe, leather, bold colors such as orange, burgundy, purple, bright turquoise, and rustic furniture mix well with this style, as do silver items, lassos, cactus and maybe even a saddle. Influenced by indigenous Indian and Spanish cultures, the Mexican and Southwestern styles are earthy, sophisticated and soulful. Furniture is rough-and-ready wood with decorative carvings; wool textiles are hand-woven with geometric motifs of nature; light fixtures are ornamental tin and wrought iron. The Southwestern adobe style exudes a peaceful panache with subdued tones of surrounding mesas.

Traditional or Early American is a perfect motif for log homes because it reinforces the timelessness that inspires many people to choose one in the first place. The American Colonial style from 1730 to 1790 blends classical English Georgian elements and indigenous American contributions for a relaxed, traditional feel. Because wood was so appreciated, pieces are marked by attention to grain and color, and feature inlays of contrasting wood. This style leans heavily on antiques and reproductions, but because of the informality of a log home, the pieces that work best are the ones that look inviting, not stuffy.

Arts & Crafts (also called **Mission**) extols furniture with simple lines whose appeal is its wood grains and tones. As a result, it goes extremely well with logs. The popularity of this style has prompted contemporary reproductions. Mahogany, cherry and walnut are favored woods for Arts & Crafts furniture, and their rich tones can clash with mid-range log colors.

Contemporary applies to almost any piece of furniture that doesn't fall into a stylized design. It is marked by comfort and conservatism, with simple lines and a variety of fabrics. Contemporary pieces go well with any log style and mix with other furniture styles, provided you watch your color coordination. Patterns are bold and bright, while using a lightly colored background, neutral coloring for furniture and bright splashes of color in accessories. The Contemporary style honors current living and values. Interiors are functional, physically comfortable, environmentally conscious and versatile.

All of these styles can prove helpful in pulling together a look. Best of all, because log-home decor tends to be informal, you can mix elements of different styles.

Now is a good time to discuss the prevalent scheme commonly called eclectic. Selecting a variety of pieces with no apparent relationship takes particularly good judgment. There is a fine line between true eclectic and hodgepodge. Pieces that are assembled haphazardly will end up competing with each other—and with your log walls—for attention. The constant clash will make the room unsettling to be in.

Earlier, I mentioned that logs impose texture and color, making log walls more than mere backdrops. In ordinary homes, people decorate walls with paint and wallpaper. These elements establish a general mood, which the furniture embellishes. If you decide you want different furniture, you can simply paint or paper the walls. In a log home, it is important to integrate the walls into your furniture theme. That is why you see so much wood in log homes.

In this sense, decorating and designing a log home are the same process. The size and shape of the logs you choose will establish the overall look of your home. The particular wood species you prefer will add a distinctive grain pattern to your rooms. Stains can change the color of your logs, but the grain remains.

If you decide to add color, coordinate it with the logs. That doesn't mean it has to be muted earth tones. Wood works well with nearly every color. Just remember that the very lightest and very darkest woods work best with vibrant colors, whereas the natural red hue of many species is enhanced by softer tones and neutral colors.

A log home can have painted and papered walls, of course, wherever you choose to have stud-framed interior partition walls. Many two-story log homes have log walls for the first floor but conventionally framed walls for the second level. This arrangement saves money and adds variety to the decorating possibilities. Likewise, finished basements are a place to provide contrast to the wall logs.

But the walls of your major rooms will be log; otherwise, why would you have chosen to live in a log home in the first place? Here are some factors that will direct your furnishings.

- The logs themselves are a key element of any decor. Fortunately, logs go well with a wide variety of furniture styles, especially those rooted in the American tradition. They tend to clash with the ornate and frilly.
- The open space in many log-home layouts requires attention to provide visual distinction of the various areas. Use cues and groupings.
- Hand in hand with openness is volume. Log homes generally have a grander scale than conventional homes, especially if you favor today's popular high ceilings. One of the most glaring incongruities in a new log home occurs when people furnish it with pieces from their previous home. No matter how nice these pieces look, in the context of a room with volume, they suddenly appear totally out of place, certainly dwarfish and possibly laughable.
- If your log home enjoys a particularly scenic setting, windows can bring the view into your home and become part of the interior. The most overriding concern in furnishing a log home is the light. Wood is like a sponge where light is concerned. True, the knock against log homes—that they are dark and dreary abodes—no longer prevails. But they remain either darker than ordinary homes with white walls, or else they have become so filled with natural light, thanks to the huge windows and skylights that are in vogue, that the challenge is to mute its effects.
- Sunlight quickly fades bright fabrics, yet nothing awakens a log-home interior like a splash of color. Even though wood has its charms, the combination of wood walls, wood floors and wood furniture can become tiresome without some relief.
- A great way to add color and balance the light in a log home is houseplants. The greenery provides a natural complement to wood.
- Red and blue will enliven any setting. Patterns, whether simple or elaborate, enhance wood wonderfully. Toss an Oriental rug in a room with nothing but wood, for example, and the space suddenly seems

vibrant. This same energy prevails when you choose colorful plaids and patterns for upholstery.

▶ Leather is popular as upholstery because it goes so well with wood. What's more, it is durable and attractive. Leather-covered pieces also tend to be built on a scale that matches the volume of today's high-ceiling great rooms.

If you have trouble determining the relationship of different items to each other or the appropriateness of certain pieces, or if the whole prospect of decorating a log home makes you more anxious than excited, don't fret. Hire a pro.

Good decorators will work with you, involving you in the process and educating you along the way. The best decorators will take you on shopping

trips with them and encourage your developing confidence, sometimes to the point where you may wonder why you hired them in the first place. But, of course, without them, you never would have achieved this confidence.

However you choose to furnish your log home, the following strategy will assure that everything works together.

Start by thinking about the room's function. Consider how a room or space will be used, then decorate it so that form follows function. Moving into a new home does allow you the opportunity to reassess your lifestyle, but don't expect to change old habits. If you aren't the entertaining type, moving into a log home isn't likely to prompt you to start throwing regular parties.

Build intimacy through cozy groupings. It's important to arrange furniture so that it's conducive to conversations, especially if you have a very big room. Different types of rugs can be used to define the seating groups and unify the decor in a room. Art and accessories also work.

Use colors and textures. Once the room is laid out as a functional living space, colors and textures set the tone. Inviting, warm colors and textures, for instance, are the essence of Western design, which is based on living with the land and the environment. These include earth tones such as brown, green and dark red, as well as the primaries, and textures such as wood grain and rock.

Let textiles help. Fabric and weavings also help set the scene, whether used as an element of the furnishings or as stand-alone pieces. Pillows, window treatments and quilts hung over a railing are other ways to introduce textiles.

Create the mood with lighting and accessories. Lamps and sconces are particularly good choices for setting the scene. Lighting can help define spaces and reinforce the decor theme you've chosen. Keep in mind that locations of wall-mounted sconces need to be determined when the log walls are being set.

Follow your heart. If all else fails, do what you want to do. It's amazing how much taste and style most people have if they trust their instincts and not what somebody else thinks they should do.

You'll need to decide what you already own that might fit in. If you're changing your primary residence from a non-log to a log home, a lot will usually transfer. Or you may have the wherewithal to start from scratch. That'll certainly be the case with a second home.

The main reason furniture from your existing home might not work is that it's very likely out of scale with your log home. If that's the case and money is tight, at least spend what you can for two items: a new sofa for the living room and a new bed for the master bedroom. A larger-scale sofa, ideally with at least one complementary chair, will establish themselves as the centerpiece of your new home, allowing other pieces to flourish in supporting roles. Likewise, you've been dreaming of your new master suite, which will be your sanctuary, and there's your old bed, looking dwarfed and dinky. Even if you keep the same beat up old mattress, get a new bed frame that matches the scale of the room and a new bedspread. ✿

28 Landscape for Beauty and Wildlife

Turning your attention to outside the home, planning your setting should be a big part of your home's design. Strive to make your yard as livable as your home. Planning the surroundings affects the appearance as much as the color, size and shape of the house do. Remember, too, that your living space doesn't end at the front door. Determining how you will use your land is just as important as deciding upon the impression you want to make. You don't want to create a pretty picture that is impossible to keep going.

Maybe you've always wanted a gazebo or a prized rose garden and think this is finally the right time. It is. But before you begin staking it out, answer four vital questions regarding your property:

- How much of your home budget have you set aside for landscaping and out-buildings, as well as future work on the property?
- How much time can you give to building and maintaining the property?
- Have you thought about the local wildlife and how your landscaping will affect them—and you?
- How much time will you actually spend outdoors just enjoying what you've created?

The last question is often overlooked, but it is very critical. If all your property represents is a lot of work, you'll never appreciate it. The grounds shouldn't—and don't have to be—drudgery. If that's the way it's going to be, it will detract from your overall enjoyment of your log home.

Better to keep things simple and well planned than to drive yourself to distraction trying to maintain a showplace. After all, you want to impress yourself more than you do anyone else. And if the log home is your second residence, you want either a really good grounds crew or a maintenance-free existence so that when you arrive at your getaway a mountain of yard work doesn't confront you.

"Our goal was to have woods and a pond. Since we couldn't find both, we decided it would be easier to plant trees than to dig a pond."

Schert Family
Hebron, Illinois

If time or money prevents you from doing all the outdoor work you want to do immediately, consider doing it in stages. Landscaping close to the house should be completed first as it provides the finishing touch. Front yards present curb appeal, so save the back yard for Phase Two, if necessary. Still, it should be ahead of outbuildings, decorative fences

and ponds. Creating a getaway on your property to enjoy the outdoors is better for the tired soul than adding the extra touches.

When determining your budget, don't underestimate. Get prices from nurseries, home improvement centers or other sources so that you arrive at realistic costs. If you are moving into a secluded, wooded area, you probably will want to selectively remove trees and brush—a relatively low-cost chore, especially if you're willing to tackle the job yourself. But if you are looking to go to the max—tiered pools, picket fences and a boat dock—you need to consider not only the initial cost, but also the upkeep. Periodic painting and staining require labor, too—yours or someone else's—as well as materials, so even if you can put off the up-front cost, you have to keep in mind that every additional feature also represents increased expenditures down the road.

You can hold down the costs if you are willing and able to do at least some of the work yourself. However, an arthritic homeowner who tries putting in a 20-by-20-foot flowerbed may quickly wish she had chosen evergreens instead. With the variety of leaf colors and shapes available, it's possible to create an eye-catching garden while keeping maintenance to a minimum.

If you are handy with a hammer and have the time, go wild with lattice boards or landscape timbers. But if you have a high-pressure job that leaves you with little extra energy, you might very well enjoy a yard plan that is more spread-out and employs fewer items that will require less of your time.

The point is that your property should be an oasis that meets your expectations and needs rather than anyone else's. You will increase your property value by investing in the outdoors, but realistically, well-maintained minimalist grounds are far more attractive and valuable than the poor log home with the overgrown landscaping and rundown deck.

"When we started to excavate our site, we noticed a small cactus on top of a rock. We dug in front of the cactus to a rock layer. We then brought in a backhoe and, combined with picks and shovels, dug out seven layers of limestone in shades of rose and lavender that we incorporated into our walkways and patios. By revealing the limestone layers, the home appears as if it grew out of the ground."

Hondru Family
Celadone, Colorado

Landscaping for Wildlife

There's a fine line between creating a wildlife-friendly landscape and creating an environment that puts both wildlife and people at risk.

Wildlife don't know the difference between your backyard and theirs. They don't realize they're welcome to the food you put out but that you want them to leave your prize perennials alone. Or that your bird feeder is for the birds—not the foxes, owls and hawks that dine on them. Corn meant for the deer also appeals to raccoons, coyotes, foxes, skunks and rodents.

Creating unnatural concentrations of deer, rabbits and rodents attracts all kinds of critters in the food chain, from bobcats and snakes to mountain lions. And once they learn your yard is a safe haven, many predators find unwary house pets easy pickings. Even deer or elk become much less enchanting when they devour thousands of dollars worth of landscaping.

What's the responsible thing for a wildlife lover to do? Learn what species you're sharing space with, and how to choose and situate landscaping so you can enjoy the wildlife without creating problems for the critters and yourself. And think long and hard before you start any supplemental feeding program; smart landscaping, habitat improvement and providing shelter and water can actually help you attract a wider range of species. ✿

Living in Bear Country

by Linda Masterson

Bears don't have much choice about where they live, but people do. If you choose to live in bear country, there are some simple precautions you can take to reduce the chances you'll wake up one morning and find a bear on your deck—or in your kitchen.

Bears are naturally wary of people. With a little planning, you can keep them that way. If the log home of your dreams is still just a gleam in your builder's eye, you can locate, design, build and landscape in ways that will discourage bears. If you already live in bear country, there are many simple adjustments you can make to help keep your wildlife wild.

Black bears seldom venture far from cover, as their normal response to danger is to vanish into the woods or scamper up a tree. To discourage bear exploration, pick a building site out in the open, away from meadow edges, streams and obvious wildlife trails.

If you're planning on leaving trees close to your house, keep in mind that even adult bears can scoot up trees in no time flat. Try to make sure it's not a short leap from a sturdy branch to your upstairs balcony.

If you plant a backyard smorgasbord, you can't blame bears for showing up to chow down. Avoid landscaping close to your house with fruit trees or berry-producing bushes, trees or shrubs. Plant vegetable gardens well away from any type of cover, and install an electric fence to protect your harvest. Compost piles that contain anything other than green vegetation and yard waste are notorious for attracting bears.

Bears are often attracted to our homes by things we leave outside that smell good or look familiar. Eau de garbage is a heady perfume a bear's super sensitive nose can detect from miles away. Some thought about what you're

This bear got too comfortable around people and started breaking into homes. She was eventually killed by wildlife officers.

going to do with your trash can prevent a lot of problems—for you and the bears.

Whether you have curbside pickup or take your garbage to a community dumpster or landfill, you need a secure place to stash it in between. If you must store trash outside overnight, use bear-resistant containers, an enclosed trash corral, or an electric-fenced enclosure. A sturdy outbuilding with doors and windows that lock is an even better choice.

French doors with those gracious lever handles are easy to open—for both bears and people. Although bears are very dexterous, they can't get a grip on old-fashioned round door knobs, and have more trouble with doors that open out instead of in. Windows and sliding glass doors should be double or triple paned, with sturdy locks.

Your kitchen is the heart of your home; it's also a mother lode of calories beyond a bear's wildest dreams. Waking up to the sound of the contents of your pantry crashing down onto your hand-hewn plank floors is not what most people have in mind when they say they're looking forward to getting closer to nature.

In some areas with a lot of bear activity, bears have learned that those big boxes in the kitchen are full of enough food rewards to make the risk worthwhile. It's smart to locate your refrigerator so it's not visible from outside, or install curtains or shutters that can be closed. And don't go for a walk and leave windows open and doors unlocked with several pies cooling on the counter, or you could return—as one resident of the Town of Snowmass Village, Colorado did—to piles of blueberry bear scat adorning your off-white berber carpeting, and a satisfied bear sleeping it off on the sofa.

Decks and patios are often home to barbecue grills. Grills smell like food long after the burgers are gone, so if you can design a simple way to roll your grill inside, you can avoid tempting bears.

Feeding birds in bear country requires some advance planning if you want to avoid adding *Ursus americanus* to your lifetime species list. A typical bird feeder holds an astonishing 12,000 calories worth of seed in a handy carry-out container. If you don't mind losing a feeder to the bears, consider this: after the bird seed is gone, there's always the garbage. Or the garage. Or maybe the kitchen.

Planning where and how to feed the birds while you're planning the rest of your home can

A study in New York showed that 80 percent of bears involved in complaints had their first "people equal food" experience at a bird feeder.

make bear-smart bird feeding easier. Feeders need to be hung at least 10 feet off the ground and 10 feet from anything climbable, or brought in every night during bear season. You can also create seed-free ways to attract birds, like bird baths, ponds and water features. Having your excavator dig out your pond and your electrician run wiring for the filter and pump is a whole lot easier than retrofitting it later on.

Bears are intelligent, resourceful and adaptable. Do your part to be bear smart and your bears will be the best kind of neighbors: seldom seen, and never borrowing things they have no intention of returning. ❁

The Bear Facts

▶ There are nearly a million black bears in North America, now found if all but seven states.

▶ A bear's sense of smell is seven times better than a bloodhound's and 100 times better than ours. They use their powerful noses to locate food.

▶ Bears are smarter than dogs and incredibly curious.

▶ Bears have great memories and no problem learning Tuesday is trash night.

MORE INFORMATION:

▶ *Living With Bears: A Practical Guide to Bear Country* by Linda Masterson

▶ Get Bear Smart Society *www.BearSmart.com*

▶ Your state wildlife management agency or local university

29 Have Realistic Expectations

Your log home may begin as a dream, but the only way you can make that dream come true is by having a firm grip on reality. Dream and reality occasionally clash. Time and money may seem constantly conspiring to thwart your carefully devised plans. When they do, remember that the fault isn't with the time or money, it's with your plans.

It's difficult to anticipate how events will unfold until the actual moment when they occur. Timelines require flexibility, updating, improvisation and a roll-with-the-punches attitude—what Thais philosophically term *mai pen lai* and GIs bluntly call "no sweat"—especially as the project nears completion and your impatience about moving into your new home mounts. But at almost any point in the sequence of getting your log home, obstacles can arise that dim your enthusiasm.

When they do, don't be tempted to look for shortcuts or easy answers. Allow adequate time to plan your log home, from buying your land, choosing a company, finalizing a design, hiring a builder and having the home built. Accept as you embark on this journey that there will be rough spots along the way, and when they do occur, you'll surprise yourself by not going off the deep end because you knew they were going to pop up, probably at the worst time.

This undertaking borders on the epic, but it doesn't take a miracle, just determination. Keep one thing in the forefront of your mind, however. Log homes are custom homes, and the process of building one isn't really all that different from any other custom-home project—with two exceptions. First, you have more control of the various steps leading to the home's completion. Second, log homes are built with logs.

Logs are a natural material. They're the only building material, in fact, that people romanticize, rhapsodize and fantasize about. Outside of, perhaps, the "Three Little Pigs." Folks have written songs and stories about log homes. They're in movies, on television and in commercial advertising.

Wood and its many variations are what give logs their mesmerizing character and result in the distinctive look of log homes. If you regard wood's characteristics as flaws or don't favor wood as the ultimate choice for your home, maybe you should rethink living in a log home.

Otherwise, if you're determined to live in a log home, make the commitment to buy and build yours as soon as you're able. It's easy to put off the project, but all that teaches you is how to put it off longer. Overwhelmingly, the people who enjoy living in their log home agree the rewards, the joy, the satisfaction are so great that they wish they had built theirs sooner.

When your enthusiasm slackens along the way, think back to your real goal—to live in a log home—and call to mind the image of the home you're dreaming of. That is the reality you are making happen.

Be Aware that Log Homes Aren't Just Places to Live

No matter how much people love the way their log home looks, they care more about what it represents—and that goes way beyond the actual logs and even the building. A lot of what a log home is about is the location, the land that the home sits on and is surrounded by, as well as your state of mind when you're living in a log home. More than just places to live, log homes are a way of life.

That truth is evident when you ask people why they chose to live in a log home. Their answers usually go way beyond the logs.

Living in a log home may mean getting away from it all, whether for weekends or forever. Or getting to it all. People moving to a log home from the city or suburbs say they cherish the peace and quiet that comes with living in the country. The tranquility of nature refreshes body and mind. They enjoy easy access to outdoor recreation: ski slopes, trails, boating and swimming in fresh water, observing wildlife—you name it. In fact, many people who decide not to buy a log home still go ahead with the rest of the log-home dream: moving to a rural or even a remote setting.

Such a setting offers many rewards, but they come at a price. Living in a log home may mean sacrificing easy access to shopping and many conveniences you're accustomed to. Where will you get your car serviced? Does the grocery store offer the variety you're accustomed to? As you get on in years, you may find the prospect of the nearest medical facility being an hour or so away daunting, and the fact that the rescue personnel that will be taking you there are volunteers with limited training and equipment even more worrisome.

Expecting solitude, you discover that your neighbors are way too noisy, especially the ones with lots of machinery. Or too nosy. They may be disappointing conversationalists, and you might find it harder to fit in than you reckoned, even if the construction crew that worked on your log home did spread the good word about you.

And sometimes the peace and quiet turns out to be too much to stand. More than a few log-home owners have put their homes on the market after only a year or two of living amid the natural splendor they craved because they discovered they miss the hustle-bustle.

As with so many things in life, living in a log home is a trade-off. Before you make the ultimate commitment, take a good look at what you're giving up as well as what you're gaining.

If you do remain convinced this is the move you really want to make, give yourself adequate time to adjust. Get out and about, but don't try too hard to fit in or force yourself on your new community. Just be yourself.

If from time to time your situation doesn't seem to be working well, remind yourself of your original goal: to live in a log home. That means living the log-home life. It's a new role for you, so get yourself into character and act the part. ✿

Before you make the ultimate commitment, look at what you are giving up, as well as what you're gaining.

Nature's Way

A big reason some people long to live in a log home is to get closer to nature: countryside, clear skies, clean air, birds singing, deer grazing, chipmunks chattering and all that. But nature isn't the Peaceable Kingdom. To folks moving from the city or suburbs, the country is unfamiliar territory. Woods especially can sometimes seem downright scary.

When you build your log home in the country, you're intruding on an established habitat for wildlife—and not just furry critters. When I began writing about log homes, new owners called wanting to know why flies were invading their dwellings. Was there something about the wood? Could it be the chinking or the stain? I began asking log-home experts, whose first question was, "Are the homes located in the country?" Of course they were. Where else would you build a log home? Flies, it turns out, like country living, too. They regard any home as a source of food and shelter. Their appearance has little to do with a home's being log and lots to do with its being in the country.

Homes built in or near the woods are objects of curiosity for all manner of bugs, which, unlike raccoons and bears, have an amazing ability to find their way into a seemingly impenetrable house. The best way to discourage flies and other insects is to make sure your house is sealed tight. Caulk and seal every possible opening and crack, around doors and windows, log joints and especially where the roof and walls intersect—i.e., under the eaves. Some will still get through the barrier, but console yourself that most insects are harmless to you and your home. You have to learn to live with them, just as they learn to live with you.

A second, far greater threat for woodland homes is wildfires. These conflagrations are a recurring threat out West, where forests are vast and the weather is dry, but they pose a danger anywhere where trees stand and rain hasn't fallen in a while.

Logs rarely burn. It takes a tremendous amount of heat to ignite them. So your best defense is to keep heat away from your logs.

▶ Build your house with nonflammable materials, especially the roof, which is the most vulnerable part of any home in a wildfire's path. A metal or treated roof will reduce the chances of fire spreading to your home.

▶ Create defensible space around your home by thinning the nearby trees and clearing out all underbrush that could stoke the flames.

▶ Have a source of water nearby. In the country, this usually means a pond rather than a fire hydrant. You'll need a pump and hose to carry the water from its source to douse your house.

A fourth, crucial step is to plan an escape route. If all else fails, your survival is imperative. ✦

30 Move In and Move On

Knowing exactly what you'll be getting and what you're getting into when you decide you want to live in your very own log home will tremendously improve your chances of reaching your goal. As I mentioned at the outset, based on what so many other log-home owners have told me, after you have survived the buying-and-building process, the glitches and aggravations you experienced as the home was being built will prove negligible—if you even remember them at all. Instead, you will likely look back upon the construction of your log home as one of the great adventures of your life. Make the most of it.

Once you're settled in your new log home, even any spats you had with each other and disputes you had with your builder will become part of the story you'll grow fond of telling. Trust me, you will develop a story about your log home because just about everyone else does. You may even give your log home a name.

To help you craft your narrative and remind yourself of what you have accomplished, as soon as you are comfortably living in your log home, review your journal, blogs and photos. It's easy to get caught up in the day-to-day progress as it unfolds and lose sight of all that you've accomplished getting from gathering ideas to furnishing and landscaping your finished home. A detailed review will go a long way toward deepening your appreciation of your log home. If nothing else, it'll make for a great year-end holiday newsletter. And you'll have no problem coming up with a photo for that year's Christmas card.

You may have discovered as you were considering a log home how willingly other log-home owners you met told you their story or even invited you to come see their home. I've always marveled at the nerve of some people to knock on the door of a log home they've spotted and ask the owner if they can look inside. Believe me, I've heard about that happening dozens of times. But what amazes me even more is the eagerness of the owners to invite these strangers in for a tour. Sometimes they even feed their unexpected guests. I suspect that sometimes the guests aren't totally unexpected. Log homes just seem to invite company.

You probably won't believe this, but I promise it's true. A fair number of log-home owners told me they've actually become good friends with their builder. Same with their log-home sales rep. It isn't really that strange. They're all members of the same communities: the one where they physically live and the one that loves log homes.

Log-home owners are a different breed, that's for sure. They live so apart from each other and generally everyone else, and yet they feel and express camaraderie with each other that is reassuring in this day and age. Photographers and writers I've worked with over the years all tell tales of having been invited to come stay at the homes, sometimes even when the owners aren't around. I've experienced that hospitality myself.

A number of log-home owners say they chose a log home because they felt a connection, usually to the log-home tradition or to the romantic image or to the way of life that log homes represent in North America. Part of that connection is toward those who share this sentiment.

The American frontier long ago disappeared, having fulfilled its Manifest Destiny, and yet the sense of adventure, achievement and community that characterized the settling of this continent seems very much alive among log-home owners. Living in a log home cannot help but draw you to that pioneer spirit and all it represents.

When you have completed your log home, you will join the more than half a million families that are living their dream. Being one in only a half-million ought to make you feel very special indeed. ❀

Preserve Your Home's Good Looks

Congratulations. You are now well prepared to become the proud owner of a new log home. Once it's built, all you have to do is enjoy it. Oh, and protect it. Your perfectly planned log home has the potential to endure a hundred years or more. A little care on your part will ensure it lasts that and longer.

Logs need protection because they aren't trees any more than leather is a cow. Bereft of life, logs are inclined to decay. Delaying decay requires intervention to protect logs against the elements and from wood's natural enemies.

Prompted by irresponsible log-home companies claiming as recently as 20 years ago that log homes are maintenance-free, the Log Homes Council (*www.loghomes.org*) has sponsored extensive research into the wood maintenance and preservation. Its findings and recommendations are available not just to its member companies, but also to non-members and to consumers. A downloadable PDF of its *Preservation & Maintenance of Log Structures* found in the Log Home Library on its web site is available to amplify this summary of its main points.

Log homes require no more maintenance than other types of wood-sided homes. Usually less, in fact, because, unlike homes with wood or any other siding, the logs themselves make up the structural soundness of the building. That means there's no internal framing that could be harboring trouble.

A log house is like a big piece of furniture that requires dusting or washing of the interior log walls and beams every year or two. Sealed logs make the job much easier.

Anything about to go wrong with your logs will be evident on the outside, where you can spot it and deal with it before it becomes a problem. You only need to be aware of factors that might predispose your logs to various threats.

Climate affects the expected life of wood exposed to the weather. According to the USDA Forest Products Laboratory, the most severe location in the United States for wood decay is the Southeast, where rainfall is high and the weather is warm and humid. In the Northeast and Midwest, decay advances at a somewhat slower rate. In the Northwest, the decay hazard is moderate near the coast but can be severe on the coast. Decay is less hazardous in most of the Southwest because the region is very dry. In mountainous regions, localized areas with marked differences in temperature and rainfall occur.

Once trees are cut and the bark removed, logs urgently need outside protection. Wood is constantly changing moisture content with humidity and temperature changes in its environment, absorbing and releasing moisture. Wood in service is also a natural food source for several species of insects and fungi, and provides shelter and nests for other creatures.

Wood-digesting insects or fungi require four conditions to survive:

- ▶ **Food**: Polysaccharides and other carbohydrates that make up the wood cell wall.
- ▶ **Temperature**: Organisms thrive between 68 and 97 degrees F. Molds and sap stains grow between 75 and 85 degrees.
- ▶ **Oxygen**: Decay organisms require 20 percent free oxygen in the wood.
- ▶ **Water**: Decay organisms require 28 to 30 percent moisture content in the wood, but some fungi can survive and discolor (stain) the wood

with as little as 20 percent. Unprotected wood left in contact with water will absorb moisture to near fiber saturation (25 to 20 percent MC). In higher relative humidity, the wetted wood dries slowly, allowing the wood to decay for a longer period.

Although eliminating any or all of these conditions will end the threat, we can control only two: water and food (the wood itself).

Water

Moisture in logs comes from two sources. One is original moisture from the tree that remains in the incompletely seasoned log. The other is moisture that enters dried wood from the environment.

Water occurring naturally in the wood is referred to as its initial moisture content. Moisture content (MC) is expressed as a percentage of its dry weight. Don't fret over how it's calculated, unless you're embarking on a study of wood technology. Instead, be satisfied with understanding how a log's MC changes and the implications of those changes.

Some discussions of MC suggest that the figure is absolute and permanent. It isn't and varies. Due to the large cross sections of logs used to build homes, for instance, the wood near the surface may be drier than the wood closer to the center.

A log's moisture content is significant for several reasons:

▶ Wood will continue to lose moisture through evaporation until it reaches equilibrium with the temperature and relative humidity of the surrounding environment. This MC—known as the equilibrium moisture content, or EMC—varies with the small, day-to-day fluctuations in the temperature and humidity and with the large seasonal differences in these two factors.

Higher humidity raises the moisture content. At any given humidity level, the higher the temperature, the lower the MC.

▶ Dimensional change is likely to occur due to this initial loss of moisture, called seasoning, during which cell walls shrink and become denser. The release of the stress created when the cells collectively shrink may be heard as a loud pop or seen as a crack, or check, running along the grain on the log surface. Checks typically extend radially to the heart of the log. Upward-facing checks will collect rain and must be protected from water entry or treated to eliminate the detrimental potential of water sitting in the log.

▶ Wood will also shrink and swell after reaching an initial EMC as the atmosphere around the wood changes in temperature and relative humidity. This shrinking and swelling seen in seasoned wood in service is known as movement and is familiar to anyone who has experienced sticking doors and loosened furniture joints.

▶ Discoloration by sap-staining fungi can occur when higher MC combines with seasonal high temperatures. This condition is much less of a problem during the cooler seasons and in dry climates.

▶ Wood's physical properties benefit as MC is reduced. Less moisture means lower weight and easier handling. Outer cells take stains and other treatments better. Interior sanding quality improves and becomes easier.

Some suppliers include wood-preservative treatments with their management of moisture. Pressure-treating or dip-treating processes, described below, require sufficient MC (usually above 20 percent) for proper diffusion of the preservatives into the wood.

Food

EPA-registered wood preservatives are designed to make the wood unsuitable as a food source. Many log-home companies use pressure treatments or dip treatments and apply or recommend topical treatments to protect the wood. These preservatives prevent decay and kill insects that ingest wood.

◗ Pressure treatment is a way of forcing preservatives deep into the structure of the wood cells. The logs are placed in a cylinder that is sealed, then filled with a treatment solution, usually borates (the solution may include other treatments, such as a biocide). The solution is pressurized in the cylinder to achieve maximum absorption and penetration of the preservative.

◗ Dip treatment involves submersing the logs in a water-borne solution. Dip treatments often combine biocides for surface treatment of fungi with preservative salts in the solution. These processes must balance the temperature of the solution, concentration of the salts (while maintaining them in solution), compatibility with biocides and other treatments, and submersion time. This balance affects how effectively the salts diffuse throughout the cross-section of the wood.

If your logs haven't been treated before they're delivered, you or your builder can apply a topical treatment at the job site. Topical treatments include biocides, preservatives, brighteners and other applications that are sprayed or brushed onto the surface of the wood. Most topical treatments are limited to protecting the outer layer of cells, up to a quarter-inch deep.

Besides fungi and insects, the effects of the weather can cause wood and wood finish degradation. Depending on the wood species, this surface erosion can wear away up to a quarter-inch of wood per century. Factors to be concerned with are:

◗ **Ultraviolet Light**. The sun's UV rays break down the lignin in wood cells, causing color changes and weakening surface wood fibers. Lighter woods tend to darken or turn gray, while dark woods bleach out gray. This color change is natural and affects wood's appearance, not its structure. If you find it unappealing, apply pigmented stains regularly to block the UV rays.

◗ **Moisture**. Wood swells and shrinks in response to humidity and water from rain runoff or melting snow. The repeated wetting by roof runoff splashing off a deck onto the log wall is a typical area of concern. Use good design and a water-repellent coating to keep your logs dry.

◗ **Temperature**. Increased temperatures accelerate UV deterioration. For log homes, elevated surface temperatures increase the rate of moisture evaporation within the logs, thereby causing more checking. Subsequent freezing and thawing of absorbed water contributes to checking and cracking as well.

◗ **Abrasion**. The mechanical action of wind, sand and dirt can be a factor in the rate of surface degradation and removal of wood or exterior finish material. Windblown particles can have a sandblasting effect.

Shielding the home from moisture will help combat decay in walls and foundations and around doors and windows. You can achieve protection by taking preventive steps. Start with your building site and home design, as discussed in the chapter *Design for Protection*. You can follow other steps as your home is being built and after its construction.

During construction, make certain that the attic

Linseed oil—a primary ingredient in many log home finishes—is organic, which means it likes to grow black mold in wet areas.

---

and crawl space are adequately vented to prevent moisture from accumulating within the living space. If you have a crawl space, cover the soil with polyethylene to reduce the relative humidity of the air in sub-floor spaces.

To prevent mold and mildew, when your logs are delivered, prevent them from touching the ground or each other by placing spacers between them to allow air circulation between the logs. The procedure will also help relieve any build up of moisture and heat caused by the drying logs, thereby reducing the chances of fungal attack. Be sure that the stacks of material are kept covered, using lumber wrap or opaque polyethylene, and, if possible, located in a shaded area, preferably not beneath trees you hope to save after the home is built.

If you notice any mold and mildew, remove them by using products specifically designed for log-home use or treat with the following solution. Wear goggles, rubber gloves and clothing to prevent eye and skin contact; also shield plants and shrubs.

Mix 1 cup trisodium phosphate (TSP) or non-ammoniated detergent, 1 quart of household bleach and 3 quarts of warm water. Apply the solution to the affected area with a hand-pump garden sprayer, let set for 5 to 10 minutes, then pressure rinse it with clean fresh water.

After construction, control water absorption through regular maintenance with a water-repellent treatment, stain or coating. Select a product that is labeled for use on log homes and offers exceptional water resistance or water repellency and mold and mildew protection, and allows for moisture vapor transfer. Other benefits might include wood preservation, abrasion resistance and control against ultraviolet light and fading.

When using any product, follow label instructions and these recommended guidelines:

▶ Always start with a clean surface, free of mill glaze. Mill glaze can inhibit or interfere with the finish treatment. Consult your log-home company representative if you are in doubt about mill glaze and to find out the name of products that will remove it.

▶ Clean the logs with the TSP-bleach solution recommended above, or select one of the cleaning products formulated specifically for logs. Make sure that all products used are compatible with each other.

▶ Apply a protective finish.

If you're in doubt about the proper finish treatment, consult your log-home company for recommendations. Select products that are labeled specifically for use on log homes and are suitable for the geographical region where you're building, as well as the type of wood and the moisture content at the time of initial application. Some products require that the wood "season" for a certain period before application, for example; others may not.

A good quality finish ought to last between two and five years, depending on altitude, sun and weather exposure. To determine when you need to re-apply protection, check once a year to see if your wood finish is still repelling water. Hose some water on the log wall. If it beads up, the finish is working; if it doesn't, it is time to apply another coat of stain or sealer. Expect your finish to break down sooner on the south and west walls.

By following these procedures and being aware of the nature of wood, you will ensure that your log home stands up against the elements. You will also keep it looking its best for many, many years to come. ❀

Sand your exterior logs (as tedious as that may be) before applying any stain or sealer. Hand-peeled or milled logs will not hold the coating after a few years.

Warranties: Buyer Be Wary

Do log-home companies offer warranties? Many do, yes. Should you buy only from a company that does? That depends on your understanding of the terms. So, the very first thing you should do when a company you're considering boasts that it offers a warranty is to read it.

Some companies offer lifetime warranties, although 25 years is the most common term. However long they're for, log-home warranties are almost always "limited." That means they cover only the material and workmanship that the log-home company provides. They do not cover the whole house or work handled by the builder or you. They do not cover products or work by other parties.

Builders cause most problems that arise with new and not-so-new log homes. Defects usually occur within the home's first four or five years. The log-home companies provide detailed construction manuals with very specific instructions, to be followed to the letter to assure that the home is built according to the engineered building system designed specifically for it. Any deviation lessens their liability. If a problem arises and your builder skipped a step, your warranty will likely be null and void, even if there is a problem with the logs. If the dispute goes to court or arbitration, the log-home company will almost surely shift the blame to your builder—or to you, if you provided your own materials or labor. That's the way warranties work, no matter how they're worded.

The few legitimate warranty claims are usually resolved quickly and amicably. Some companies belong to the Log Homes Council, which gives homeowners with a grievance a forum to complain and whose members have agreed to abide by the council's decision. The council also requires its members to meet certain standards, such as selling only logs that have been graded by a third-party agency. Council member or not, companies' biggest reason for making things right is the importance of their reputation.

If builders are often to blame for flaws because they don't follow directions, why don't log-home companies build the homes they sell? It's mostly a liability issue. Construction isn't sawmilling or even designing or delivering homes. Companies that have bowed to consumer pressure to provide full service on log homes invariably handle the construction aspect with a separate or subsidiary company that assumes liability for that part of the work. The log companies limit their responsibility only to the logs.

In many cases, they will provide crews to erect the log shell or offer technical assistance. From a liability standpoint, as well as workmanship and materials, it's in companies' best interest to assure proper assembly. Once your logs are delivered, however, they become your responsibility. If you accept them in good condition, any subsequent flaw you spot is hard to pin on the company.

You'll also find a big discrepancy between what you see as a problem and what the log-home company does. Checking (longitudinal cracking of wood), for example, is an aesthetic turn-off for some homeowners and an out-and-out defect to others. From a warranty standpoint, however, checking is part of wood's natural character. Checking results from uneven or accelerated drying of your logs. That is, if you heat your home and checking occurs, checking is your fault. Also if you build your home so constant sun dries some logs unevenly, again, that's what wood does. Other conditions that are natural characteristics of the wood, according to company warranties, are twisting, warping and certain aesthetic issues, such as discoloration, that occur after the home is built.

Exposed wood has to be protected. Even if your

log-home company sold or gave you wood stain that was supposed to protect your logs from the sun's rays, liability lies with the stain maker unless the stain manufacturer argues you didn't follow directions when you applied the stain.

It's the same situation with windows and doors that come with your package. Maybe also roofing shingles, floor joists or structural insulated panels used to cover your roof. The log-home company's warranty extends only to its own work and materials. It mills the logs and assures that the logs are appropriate for the building as designed.

A typical warranty makes no provision for air leakage through doors, windows, vents or other openings other than the log-wall assembly. Finally, most warranties state that in case of defect, the company reserves the right to choose how to resolve the problem, whether by refund, replacement or repair.

What good, then, is a warranty? It's a token of good faith intended to give you peace of mind.

More important than a document that probably won't hold up in court is the track record of log-home companies. Since the mid-1980s, thousands of log homes have been built every year. Some have had problems that log-home companies have fixed, even problems that weren't their responsibility. As a whole, the log-home industry strives to provide quality materials that perform for many years. It is in the industry's best interest to satisfy customers and meet high standards.

Fortunately, only a handful of companies have questionable ways of doing business, and there is no history of fly-by-night log producers. A few companies have failed while holding deposits for homes never delivered or even cut, but for the most part other companies have stepped in to buy the inventory, including open orders, and have either honored deposits, settling for the balance due, or negotiated terms under the circumstances. Financial well-being and track record aren't warranty issues. Neither is hassles affecting delivery of the materials, only the materials themselves—with limitations.

Some log-home companies offer third-party warranties—for example, by Residential Warranty Corporation—that cover problems beyond those specified by the log-home company's own warranty. These warranties usually provide for a deductible, to be paid by the homeowner in the event of a claim. If this is the case with the company you're considering, make sure you read and understand the scope of the coverage.

The best way to deal with warranties is to preempt them by understanding thoroughly how wood in use behaves. Make sure your builder comprehends how your home is to be assembled and follows directions to the letter. And make sure you maintain your logs as required. By following these best practices, you'll most likely never have any problems that would raise the issue of your warranty. ❁

How Your Log Home Happens

It's exciting to look at land you just bought and imagine your log home sitting right there on it, setting the stage for the next chapter in your life. Getting that log home is sure to wind up a big part of the story. You're clearly the main character where it tells about buying your log home. That includes designing it, which can be the most fun, thinking of the possibilities.

When you get to the part about actually building the home, though, unless you've already built a log home, the yarn turns into a mystery—a real how-done-it. You may find yourself demoted to a supporting character.

Whatever your role in the narrative, everyone wants to know how their story turns out. This timeline gives a good plot outline and sorts out the different characters.

Don't wait to find out the ending, though. This schedule of events can help you preview your project, letting you work backwards from completion so you can plan when best to start. And if you're considering the role of general contractor, you can survey the undertaking.

The building sequence remains pretty much the same for all log homes, although times obviously vary, usually from six months to two years. The average is about a year. Add or subtract for complexity or simplicity of design. Two unquantifiable variables remain: the weather and unanticipated circumstances.

Taking all these factors into account, here is a reasonable estimate of events that will unfold to become your log home. Note that many of the steps are the same for a log home as they are for an ordinary home. Also, in most cases, although the general contractor doesn't perform the actual work, she's responsible for making sure everything is ready for the subcontractor, scheduling the sub in proper sequence and making sure the necessary inspections are completed.

Activity	Who's Responsible
Acquire a complete set of blueprints	Homeowner
Obtain building permits	General contractor (GC)
Site preparation & road work	Excavator: Basic site prep includes providing access for heavy equipment that will clear the site. Identify a way from the road to the site and clear the route of trees and topsoil. The road building continues with a stone bed capable of supporting pickup trucks, concrete trucks, cranes and tractor-trailers delivering the logs and other materials, as well as any culverts.
Arrange for insurance, temporary electricity, temporary telephone service (crucial if cell-phone reception is spotty) and portable toilets	General contractor

Activity	Who's Responsible
Drill water well and install pump	Well driller
Install septic tank and drain (leach) field	Septic contractor
Excavate for foundation	Excavator: The excavator digs a pit or levels an area for the foundation.
Dig and prepare footings	Foundation contractor: Footings support the foundation and weight of the house and must be located below the frost line.
Install under-foundation pipes for utilities	Plumber: Besides making sure workers will have access to pipes after the home is built, the plumber installs pipes and drains that will run under the basement floor.
Pour concrete footing and pier pads	Foundation contractor
Termite protection	Exterminator
Install forms for poured-concrete foundation	Foundation contractor: Poured-concrete foundations are popular for log homes with basements, but foundations may also be masonry block, pre-cast concrete panels or wood. Part of the foundation work is providing adequate drainage around the base of the foundation wall.
Pour concrete foundation	Foundation contractor: If the home will have a masonry or stone fireplace, the foundation contractor will see that footings and walls are prepared to support the additional weight.
Waterproof foundation	Foundation contractor: A waterproof coating is usually applied to foundation walls.
Backfill around foundation	Excavator: The excavator will also rough grade a slope for the lawn that ensures water will drain away from the foundation.
Install subflooring system: I-beams, support posts, joists, and oriented strand boards (OSB)	Builder

Activity	Who's Responsible
Delivery of log-home package	General contractor and log-home company representative: The GC makes sure that delivery trucks can access the site and turn around to exit after dropping off their load. The GC will also arrange for any necessary equipment to unload the logs and for a place to store the logs and related materials that offers protection and easy access for workers. Lastly, the GC will check materials against the shipping manifest to make sure everything is delivered and arrange to have any missing items shipped promptly.
Erect the log walls	Builder or company rep: Some log-home companies dispatch their own crew to erect a weathertight log shell, a task that rarely takes more than a few days. At that point, the builder takes over. If no crew is scheduled, the builder will erect the home according to the log-home company's detailed construction manual. Electrical wiring may need to be considered at this stage.
Frame gable ends, dormers, etc.	Builder
Install roof system and sheathing	Builder: Depending on your ceiling design, insulation may be installed at this point.
Install exterior windows and doors	Builder
Frame interior walls, stairs and loft floor	Builder
Install rough plumbing system	Plumbing contractor: This step also includes roof penetrations for vent pipes, flues, etc.
Install rough heating, ventilation and air conditioning (HVAC) ductwork and equipment	HVAC contractor / plumber
Install roofing felt, flashing and shingles	Roofing contractor
Erect fireplace and chimney	Masonry contractor
Apply exterior stain and preservatives to logs	Painter: Sealing the exterior is crucial for protecting the logs. Look for products especially formulated for wall logs.

Activity	Who's Responsible
Apply stain and/or sealant to interior log walls	Painter
Apply interior and exterior chinking and caulking	Chinking and caulking contractor: Be sure everything is well sealed to prevent heat loss.
Install soffits, fascia, frieze and rake boards	Builder
Install exterior window and door trim	Builder
Install rough electrical wiring and service panel	Electrical contractor: Building code may require the house to be sealed up before any wiring is done.
Install final HVAC equipment and test	HVAC contractor
Pour concrete floors, driveways and walkways	Concrete contractor
Insulate ceiling and interior walls	Builder
Install gypsum wallboard and tape	Drywall contractor
Install interior doors and hardware	Builder
Install interior window and door trim	Builder
Apply interior paint, stain and wall coverings	Painter
Install hardwood flooring, resilient or ceramic tile, and padding and carpeting	Flooring contractor
Install cabinets and countertops	Builder
Tile bathroom showers, walls, countertops	Builder
Install vanities, towel bars, soap dishes, mirrors, medicine cabinets, tub and shower doors, etc.	Builder
Install plumbing fixtures and appliances; connect to well water and test	Plumber
Install closet shelves, poles and hardware, drapery rods, misc. hardware	Builder

Activity	Who's Responsible
Install stair treads, railings and balusters	Builder
Install electrical fixtures, appliances, outlet covers and switch plates	Electrical contractor
Install rock or stucco or other finish on gables, foundation walls, etc.	Builder
Install porch / deck floor boards	Builder
Install porch ceilings, posts, stairs and railings	Builder
Install gable louvers and soffit vents	Builder
Stain / paint exterior trim	Painter
Install gutters and downspouts	Roofing contractor
Hookup permanent utilities	Phone & cable / satellite TV = Homeowner Water & septic = Plumber Natural gas / propane = Plumber Electricity = Electrician
Finish landscaping grading, seeding, sodding and planting shrubbery	Landscaper
Building inspection	General contractor: Items to be accomplished before the home is ready for occupancy include: inspect all work by subcontractors, make a punch list of deficiencies and review with appropriate subs; reinspect building after corrections; obtain lien waivers and approve final payments; call for final building inspection; obtain certificate of occupancy; notify lender of completion; notify insurance company of completion and switch insurance to homeowner's policy; notify any other agencies of completion.

Cost-Estimating Checklist

What's eye opening is how little the cost of a log home has to do with logs, even though they make up the bulk of the material. Because of the sheer number of ingredients, people often have trouble imagining what their log home will cost. To assist your budgeting, use this worksheet to record material and labor estimates / bids. Your log-home company sales representative and general contractor can help. If you're considering acting as your own GC, this worksheet will provide a reasonable overview of what's involved.

I recommend photocopying this checklist and getting two to four bids on every line item to arrive at a fair estimate of your real cost. Just make sure the bids are for the same level of material and degree of completeness. If you spot a big discrepancy, ask each bidder for clarification. If the discrepancy persists, list the highest figure as your final estimate. Better safe than sorry.

COST ITEM	ESTIMATE
LAND COST	
Finding a building lot	
Preliminary inspection & fees	
Cost of raw land or lot	
SUBTOTAL	
PRELIMINARY BUILDING COSTS	
Survey	
Plot plan	
Percolation test (for septic)	
Engineering fees	
Legal fees	
Title & recording fees	
Taxes	
Building permits	
Other permits & fees	
Temporary living quarters	

continued

COST ITEM	ESTIMATE
Temporary services:	
Electricity	
Water, sewage, toilets	
Telephone	
SUBTOTAL	
LOAN COSTS	
Bank inspection fees	
Bank appraisal fees	
Bank assumption fees	
Credit approval fees	
Loan fees	
Interest costs	
SUBTOTAL	
INSURANCE COSTS	
Title insurance	
Public liability	
Builder's risk	
Worker's compensation	
Fire, theft, vandalism	
Vehicle, equipment	
Bonds	
SUBTOTAL	
SITE PREPARATION	
Clear site, tree removal	
Soil test	
Establishing benchmarks	
Rough grading	
Entrance road or driveway	
Bridge	
Fence & gates	
SUBTOTAL	

COST ITEM	ESTIMATE
EXCAVATIONS	
Remove & stockpile top soil	
Cut, fill & grade	
Mass excavation:	
Basement	
Septic tank	
Septic field	
Swimming pool	
Lake or dam	
Trenches:	
Sewer lines	
Septic (leach) field	
Water	
Radon Mitigation	
Electric cables	
Telephone & TV cables	
Backfill foundation	
SUBTOTAL	
FOUNDATION	
Concrete, block or wood	
Waterproofing	
Insulation	
Labor	
SUBTOTAL	
PERMANENT UTILITIES	
Heat (propane, oil, gas, electricity)	
Electricity	
Telephone	
Cable or satellite television	
Water line & tap fee	
Sewer line & tap fee	
Water well & permits	
Septic system & permits	
SUBTOTAL	

COST ITEM	ESTIMATE
CONCRETE & FORMWORK	
Footings (house & garage)	
Pier pads	
Foundation walls	
Concrete floors & steps	
Sidewalks & driveways	
Patios	
Swimming pool	
Culverts & drains	
SUBTOTAL	
FLOOR SYSTEM	
Post & columns	
Beams & girders	
Termite shield	
Sill plates	
Joists & joist hangers	
Headers & bridging	
Subflooring	
Labor / Installation	
SUBTOTAL	
EXTERIOR WALLS	
Log package:	
Materials	
Freight / delivery	
Assembly	
Sales tax	
Gable-end wall package	
Wall framing	
Sheathing	
Building paper, vapor barrier	
Siding: brick, stone, stucco, masonry, half logs	
Labor / Installation	
SUBTOTAL	

COST ITEM	ESTIMATE
GARAGE/CARPORT	
Garage / carport log wall package and assembly	
Wall framing, drywall, finish	
Fire protection, separation wall	
Garage doors	
Electronic controls, door opener	
SUBTOTAL	
ROOF SYSTEM & MATERIALS	
Rafters or trusses	
Purlins, collar ties & bracing	
Ridge board or beam	
Vents	
Dormer framing	
Skylight framing	
Sheathing	
Flashing	
Roofing felt paper	
Roofing material (roll roofing, shingles, tiles, metal roof, other)	
Labor / Installation	
Lightning protection	
SUBTOTAL	
PORCHES, BALCONIES, DECKS & PATIOS	
Floor support system	
Flooring or decking	
Posts & columns	
Balusters & railings	
Porch ceiling	
Paving stones, bricks, timbers	
Labor / Installation	
SUBTOTAL	

COST ITEM	ESTIMATE
EXTERIOR FINISH & TRIM	
Log finish (preservative, stain, sealer) & application	
Chinking, caulking	
Rake fascia, soffit & molding	
Eaves fascia, backer, trim, soffit & molding	
Soffit vents & louvers	
Frieze boards & molding	
Shutters	
Flashing	
Window & door trim boards	
Gutters, downspouts & splash blocks	
Labor / Installation	
SUBTOTAL	
INSULATION	
Ceiling	
Floors	
Walls	
Ducts & pipes	
Labor / Installation	
SUBTOTAL	
WALLS, INTERIOR	
Non-structural logs not included in the log package	
Log accents	
Wall framing (studs, plates, headers)	
Wallboard	
T & G paneling	
Labor / Installation	
SUBTOTAL	

COST ITEM	ESTIMATE
FIREPLACE & CHIMNEY	
Concrete reinforced footing	
Bricks: common, decorative, fireclay	
Concrete block	
Parget (plaster coating), mortar	
Flue lining	
Damper	
Clean out	
Ash dump	
Fuel chute	
Chimney & cap	
Flashing	
Wood stove, pellet stove, high efficiency fireplace, fireplace insert, other	
Hearth	
Labor / Installation	
SUBTOTAL	
WINDOWS	
Rough framing	
Headers, lintels	
Windows:	
House & garage	
Roof (skylights, light tubes)	
Basement	
Bay & box	
Storm windows, screens	
Labor / Installation	
Sunroom	
Greenhouses	
SUBTOTAL	

COST ITEM	ESTIMATE
DOORS, EXTERIOR & INTERIOR	
Rough framing	
Doors:	
Entrance (front, back, side)	
Balcony	
Patio	
Storm, screen	
Interior rooms	
Closets, pantry	
Attic	
Storage, mechanical room	
Labor / Installation	
SUBTOTAL	
SECOND FLOOR SYSTEM	
Post & columns	
Beams & girders	
Joists & joist hangers	
Headers	
Bridging	
Subflooring	
Labor / Installation	
SUBTOTAL	
STAIRS, INTERIOR & EXTERIOR	
To basement	
To second floor	
To attic	
Front & back entrance steps	
Deck / porch steps & stairs	
Handrails, balusters, newel posts	
Labor / Installation	
SUBTOTAL	

COST ITEM	ESTIMATE
ELECTRICAL	
Installation of wiring from point of supply (utility power or solar / wind power) to panel box	
In-house wiring for:	
Outlets, switches, dimmers	
Appliance connections	
Light fixture & ceiling fan connections	
Doorbell	
Security system, intercom	
Central vacuum	
Smoke detectors	
Attic fan	
Kitchen & bath exhaust	
Low voltage wiring (telephone, TV, computer network, sound system, etc.)	
SUBTOTAL	
HEATING & AIR CONDITIONING	
Heating system & installation	
Cooling system & installation	
Attic fan equipment	
Thermostats	
Humidifier, dehumidifier	
Air filtration system	
SUBTOTAL	
PLUMBING	
Installation of water service from point of supply to house	
Installation of sewer service from septic or sewer to house	
In-house piping: supply lines, drains, vents	
Installation of fixtures:	
Sinks in kitchen, bath, laundry	

COST ITEM	ESTIMATE
Toilets, bidets	
Washing machine	
Dishwasher	
Ice maker	
Water softener	
Bathtubs	
Hot tubs	
Showers	
Steam rooms, saunas	
Sewage disposals	
Water heaters	
Gas piping for heating system	
Solar water heating system	
Swimming pool	
SUBTOTAL	
INTERIOR FINISH & TRIM	
Floor deadening underlayment	
Finish flooring:	
Hardwood	
Carpet & padding	
Tile (resilient, ceramic)	
Brick, stone, slate	
Baseboard & shoe	
Wall molding & chair rails	
Window & door trim	
Closet shelves & hardware	
Door locks, handles, hinges	
Labor / Installation	
Stain & seal logs & woodwork	
Interior chinking & caulking	
Tape, texture & paint walls & ceiling	
Wallpapering	
SUBTOTAL	

continued

COST ITEM	ESTIMATE
APPLIANCES, CABINETS & FIXTURES	
Kitchen:	
Oven & range	
Refrigerator	
Sinks	
Dishwasher	
Garbage disposal	
Deep freezer	
Trash compactor	
Range hood	
Microwave oven	
Exhaust fans	
Cabinets	
Countertops	
Bathrooms:	
Toilets, bidets	
Bathtubs, whirlpools	
Showers	
Hot tubs	
Steam baths, saunas	
Sinks	
Vanities	
Countertops	
Medicine cabinets	
Towel bars, soap holders	
Toilet paper holders	
Bath & shower rails	
Tile (floors, walls, shower)	
Mirrors	
Laundry:	
Washer & dryer	
Sink	
Cabinets, storage	

continued

COST ITEM	ESTIMATE
Water softener	
Whole-house sound system	
Light fixtures (interior, exterior)	
Ceiling fans	
Exhaust fans, attic fan	
Central vacuum system	
Intercom, security system	
Smoke detectors	
Built-in bookshelves, cabinets	
SUBTOTAL	
FINISH & CLEANUP	
Final grading	
Landscaping	
Seeding & planting	
Interior cleaning & polish	
Removal of trash	
SUBTOTAL	
OTHER	
MOVE-IN	
Moving expense	
SUBTOTAL	
LAST EXPENSE	
Reserve for contingencies	
Large party	
SUBTOTAL	
TOTAL EXPENSE	

ACKNOWLEDGMENTS

Twenty years of writing about log homes introduced me to many people who make, sell and build these iconic dwellings. Theirs is a competitive industry, but also a collegial one. They were especially gracious in welcoming me into the club and taking time to explain what makes log homes the way they are and why. They were also helpful in introducing me to the owners of their homes who had inspiring and instructive stories to tell.

If the log-home industry is close-knit, the people who live in log homes are anything but. They're unassociated individuals all over the demographics chart, sharing pretty much only their love of log homes. That common ground was the basis of my getting to know them. They opened their doors and shared their experiences with surprising candor. To my delight, every story had a happy ending. Their success no doubt charmed many readers into realizing there is indeed something special about log homes and the people who live in them.

In telling their stories, these owners also made me aware of how formidable buying and building a log home can be. Their determination to succeed made their stories even more inspirational. The mistakes they made, the lessons they learned, the odds they overcame—all form the basis of this book.

It would be impossible for me to thank all of these log-home owners and industry people individually for their help and inspiration. Two people I would like to recognize are Stuart Good and James Murphy. They worked alongside me at many log-home shows. Their knack for getting people to open up about their log-home aspirations and frustrations made me realize that for every person who succeeded, many more failed. These show-goers' predicament made me determined to write this book.

For specific help in putting this book together, my thanks to Home Buyer Publications for granting permission to adapt several of my articles that appeared in issues of *Log Homes Illustrated*. That magazine bit the dust in 2008, but HBP publishes two venerable magazines: *Log Home Living* and *Country's Best Log Homes*. To subscribe, visit the publisher's web site: *www.loghome.com*.

For technical information pertaining to log-home care, I relied on *Preservation & Maintenance of Log Structures*, prepared by the Technical Committee of the Log Homes Council, Building Systems Councils, National Association of Home Builders. For information about log-home maintenance or other aspects of buying, building and owning a log home, visit the Council's web site: *www.loghomes.org*.

I'm grateful to the log-home companies that provided many of the photographs used throughout this book. I hope those selected for this book clearly illustrate that for everything log homes have in common, they are as different as the people who live in them.

I'm particularly indebted to LaVonne Ewing. She is the driving force behind PixyJack Press and has the ability to coax writers to write when we'd rather just think about writing than actually do it. She encouraged me that this book had merit, gave me a deadline and made sure I came tolerably close to meeting it so it could get into the hands of eager log-home buyers in time to save you time, money and frustration.

Photo Credits

COMPANIES

Appalachian Log Homes 160
  www.applog.com

Enercept 33
  www.enercept.com

Kuhns Bros. Log Homes 55
  www.KuhnsBros.com

Maple Island Log Homes
  15, 16, 63, 85, 98, 113, 119,
  127, 134, 138, 183, 189, 200
  www.MapleIsland.com

Moose Mountain Log Homes 173
  www.MooseMountain.com

MossCreek Designs / Erwin
  Loveland 62, 94, 100, 103
  www.MossCreek.net

Real Log Homes 125, 161
  www.RealLogHomes.com

Rocky Mountain Log Homes
  12, 13, 44, 61, 64, 67, 68, 76,
  77, 97, 107, 115, 145, 164,
  187, 199
  www.RMLH.com

Southland Log Homes 57, 70
  www.SouthlandHomes.com

Storm Carpenter Log Homes
  25, 120
  www.logghome.com

INDIVIDUALS

English, Michael 35

Ewing, LaVonne 36, 54, 56, 80,
  81, 165-167, 170, 176, 177

Kingsley, Linda 55, 104, 106,
  140, 150, 151

Levy, Bill 193

Phillips, Cory 31, 72

Stevens, Cindy 192

All other images courtesy of Roland Sweet.

Index

THE AUTHOR

Roland Sweet is the editor-in-chief of *Log Home Living* magazine, which he helped launch in 1989. Over the years he has also has been editor of *Log Homes Illustrated*, *Timber Homes Illustrated* and *Distinctive Wood Homes*. His book, *100 Best Log Home Floor Plans*, was released in 2007. Roland received a master's degree in magazine journalism from Syracuse University. He lives with his wife, artist Theodora Tilton, in Mount Vernon, Virginia, where he can be found hiking, flying, and compiling news of human folly, which he chronicles in a weekly syndicated newspaper column.

ALSO FROM PixyJack Press

Crafting Log Homes Solar Style:
An Inspiring Guide to Self-Sufficiency

Visit **www.PixyJackPress.com** to view
all of our renewable energy and wildlife titles
and to order autographed copies.

100% solar & wind powered since 1999

PIXYJACK PRESS INC

PO Box 149   Masonville, CO 80541 USA   www.PixyJackPress.com   info@pixyjackpress.com